W9-BMJ-736

THE COMPLETE BEGINNER'S
Guide to Golf

The Complete Beginner's Guide to Golf

BY BILL McCORMICK

WITH ILLUSTRATIONS BY
JOHN LANE

DOUBLEDAY & COMPANY, INC.
GARDEN CITY, NEW YORK
1974

ISBN: 0-385-03574-8 Trade
0-385-05529-3 Prebound
Library of Congress Catalog Card Number 73–78770

Printed in the United States of America
9 8 7 6 5 4 3 2

Contents

Contents

THE COMPLETE BEGINNER'S
Guide to Golf

CHAPTER ONE

The Game

Golf is the game for everybody.

It is one major participation sport that demands no special physical qualifications. Among the finest golfers in the world at any given time are the thin, the fat, the tiny, the huge, the strong, the weak, and the average. Bobby Jones was so puny as a child that it was feared he would not live. Billy Casper, one of the finest, is allergic to just about everything. Even the lame and the halt can play, sometimes excel. The United States Open Championship—the highest honor in golf—was won in 1954 by Ed Furgol, a professional with a shriveled arm.

Mere strength will get a player nowhere, although it can add to his playing prowess if he learns to use it properly. Women and children are on a par with men up to the limit of their physical capabilities. A woman or child with a well-developed game can easily defeat the strongest man who has not learned to play the game as he should.

Golf requires no native skill, no inherent ability. Natural-born players are scarcer than holes in one.

Most good players, including the leading professionals, are "manufactured" golfers. They have either been given good instruction at an early age, picked up the fundamentals while caddying for good golfers, or in some other way been subjected to sound teaching in the basics.

Among the immortals of the golfing world, Sammy Snead, Byron Nelson, and a host of others learned the fundamentals by imitating the swings of professionals and good amateurs for whom they caddied. A caddy as a boy, Gene Sarazen was lucky enough to come to the attention of a fine teaching pro who applied the finishing touches that made Gene the phenomenal golfer who won every major championship for which he was eligible. Bobby Jones, who started with one sawed-off club at the age of five, and Jack Nicklaus both were born into well-to-do families who gave them the benefit of the finest instruction. Arnold Palmer's father was a professional who started teaching his son almost from the time he could walk. Little Ben Hogan became an all-time great by sheer will power and application after he had been terribly injured in an automobile accident.

From time to time there does come along a maverick with great innate aptitude who manages occasionally to put together a superb round or two from completely undisciplined play. These "naturals" probably would develop into more consistently fine players if they would go back and start all over again the right way. Lee Trevino's swing, although he seems to be improving it, is awkward and unsmooth, but his wonderful coordination, strong wrists, and natural talent are enough to overcome his unorthodox swing—sometimes. Lee put everything all together in 1971 for nineteen days, during which he became practically champion of the world by winning the United States Open, Canadian Open, and British Open titles, an unprecedented accomplishment. He did it again by winning the 1972 British Open with the aid of some of the most spectacular shots ever seen.

Although it can be played by just about everyone, golf is not a mollycoddle sport. Most standard eighteen-hole courses play about three miles long as the birdie flies, but the average golfer probably will cover an additional mile or two as he zigs and zags from tee to green. The energy expended in walking, hitting the ball, and toting a bag of clubs on a round adds up to plenty of healthful exercise.

Another recommendation for golf as a principal form of recreation is that it can be played all one's life. A player does not outgrow the game. By adjusting his pace and the amount of play, a golfer can continue to enjoy and profit from the sport through ripe old age. Practically every course boasts one or two "regulars" of ancient vintage whose lean bodies, washboard tummies, and fine complexions bear witness to the lasting physical benefits of the pastime.

Forward-looking colleges are becoming more and more concerned with their students' well-being after their scholarly years. Undergraduates—even those with scholarships for such spectator sports as football and basketball—are being counseled to take up at least one participation pastime they can continue to play well beyond their school years. Golf is high on the list of lifetime sports recommended. It is something the student can take with him when he leaves school to play as often as is convenient in the world outside the academic walls. It will protect him from boredom and body bulges in later years. It will expand his social horizons. Golf even pays dividends in the business world. Many a fine job has been landed and fat deal closed on the course.

One effect of college emphasis on golf has been to introduce into the ranks of touring pros—the big boys who go after the big money in major tournaments throughout the year—a number of players who have learned or improved their games in school competition.

The game of golf had simple beginnings and remains basically a simple sport, yet it is far from easy to master. In fact, nobody quite masters it; there is always room for improvement. There is no such thing as perfection in golf (par is just an arbitrary figure, based on the length of each hole, which represents the general idea of what constitutes good golf), yet dedicated players continually strive for perfection. The duffer breaks his heart trying to break a hundred, the weekend golfer labors for scores in the nineties and eighties, and the better players grope for par or better. No matter how much the dedicated player lowers his score, he is still dissatisfied. Professionals have been known to turn in competition rounds in the low sixties, then grumble: "If only I had done this [or that or the other thing], I would have scored in the fifties!"

Although essentially a game of good cheer and conviviality, golf is in some respects a lonely sport. The player is on his own. If he gets in trouble, he can't holler for help. Playing strictly by the rules in competition, a player is not permitted even to seek advice from any but "his partner or either of their caddies." In making a stroke he cannot seek or accept "physical assistance or protection from the elements." In other words, if the course is drenched by a cloudburst while you are playing, you cannot ask someone to hold an umbrella over you while you make a shot, or even allow him to do so if he volunteers.

Perhaps a knowledge of the game's beginnings will help in understanding the true nature of golf.

The only thing known for certain about how the game started is that it was not invented. It just grew.

Historians disagree on what the sport originated from. It has been proved fairly conclusively that pre-Christian Romans played a game they called *paganica* with a forked stick and feather-stuffed ball. They may have brought the pastime to the British Isles when they invaded.

Another belief is that the game originated in Holland. There is little support for this theory beyond old drawings of Netherlanders carrying sticks with knobs at their ends, which may have been used for hitting a ball, but more likely were canes.

Golf probably started when some bored Scottish shepherd gave vent to man's inborn compulsion to hit something and send it soaring by thwacking a stone or ball of sheep fluff with his staff or some other handy stick. From this perhaps evolved a form of competition between shepherds to see who could knock an object from here to there in the fewest number of thwacks (or strokes, as they came to be called) with his stick (which developed into the modern golf club). Finally, some unsung genius conceived the idea of putting a hole at the end of the line—and golf was born. Although it has become highly refined over the centuries, the game has remained basically the same.

Wherever it came from, golf was well established in Scotland by the mid-fifteenth century, may even have been played more or less formally at St. Andrews as early as the twelfth century. The game was outlawed in Scotland in 1457 because too many men were neglecting archery practice to swat the ball, and archery was required by law as essential to the national defense.

Fortunately for the future of the sport, James IV, who ruled Scotland from 1488 to 1513, was a pretty good player and loved the game. Mary, Queen of Scots, James IV's granddaughter, learned to play in early childhood before she was sent to France to be educated. The young men who toted Mary's playing paraphernalia around the French courses were known as cadets, which is where we get our word caddy. Returning to her own country to rule, Mary indulged publicly in golf, proving that in that game all sexes are created equal and a girl doesn't have to resemble a musclemaid or a lady wrestler to be good at the pastime.

During the ban in Scotland, a bishop of St. Andrews won for his native village the right to play golf on its common links, giving the sport a permanent headquarters. The oldest golf club in the world—The Honourable Company of Edinburgh Golfers—was organized at Leith in 1744. Later, the Gentlemen Golfers, as they were called, moved to Musselburgh. There they had clubrooms in the grandstand of a race track near their playing course where they laid down the first set of rules—twelve in all—about the middle of the eighteenth century. The task of making rules was subsequently relinquished to the Royal and Ancient Golf Club at St. Andrews. In 1891, the Gentlemen Golfers moved again, this time to Muirfield, near Edinburgh on the southern shore of the Firth of Forth.

It was on the windy, often rain-swept Muirfield links that Jack Nicklaus' drive for the Grand Slam of modern golf came to grief in the British Open after the great player had won the Masters and U. S. Open in 1972.

The Royal and Ancient Golf Club was founded in St. Andrews in 1754. The Old Course at St. Andrews is possibly the most famous and unusual eighteen holes in golf. There are only nine huge double greens. Not only do outgoing (the first nine) and incoming (the second nine) holes share the same greens, they are played over the same treeless, desolate-looking fairways. The Old Course is virtually the same layout that was played by shepherds maybe eight hundred or more years ago, with bunkers in the middle of the fairway where they were wallowed out by sheep seeking protection from the strong, cold winds. Strong winds still make the comparatively short (6,951-yard) Old Course a formidable test for the best. The Royal and Ancient has made St. Andrews the mecca of all golfers.

Golf, of a sort, probably was played by the earliest settlers in the New World, but the first club was organized in the United States less than a hundred years ago. It is generally conceded to have been started by a transplanted Scot who introduced the game in a cow pasture in Yonkers, New York, during the blizzard year of 1888. From this grew a club named St. Andrews (what else?) Golf Club of Yonkers. The Yonkers club was a six-holer and gave the game the rather derogatory name of Cow Pasture Pool, which it bore in some quarters for a number of years. A year after the Yonkers project was launched, a nine-hole course was established in Middlesboro, Kentucky.

Golf was considered strictly a rich man's sport until 1913, when an unheralded caddy named Francis Ouimet won the twentieth U. S. Open Championship at Brookline, Massachusetts. The first amateur to win the coveted title, twenty-year-old Ouimet not only defeated two heavily favored British stars, Harry Vardon and Ted Ray, he did it in hand-to-hand combat, so to speak. In an eighteen-hole playoff to end a three-way tie, Ouimet scored seventy-two to Vardon's seventy-seven and Ray's seventy-eight. Those scores, which would look horrible in today's big-time competition, weren't bad at all in a time when courses and playing equipment were far less sophisticated than they are now.

Ouimet's David and Goliath victory caught the public fancy, and golf began to thrive in the United States. The next great impetus to the growth of the game came from television. Today millions of TV watchers are enthralled by the beauty of long, accurate drives from the tee, remarkable recovery shots, and long putts that find the cup over undulating greens as though guided by radar. Watchers are thrilled by the intense competition, and begin to realize how demanding the sport is when they occasionally see fine players crack up under the stress and dub shots that would seem easy to the veriest duffer.

The Game

Television offers one priceless bonus to the aspiring player: It enables him to watch and study the playing form of the very best the game has to offer and see for himself how basically simple and sound the truly efficient golf swing really is. It gives the television viewer something worthwhile to imitate, as he watches the faultless form of such sweet swingers as Jack Nicklaus and Gene Littler. Had television been around to show the youth of America the easy rhythm and precision of Bobby Jones' almost impeccable swing, there would have been a lot more good golfers in his heyday.

Although it is impossible to obtain entirely accurate figures, it is estimated that some fifteen million men, women, and children play the game regularly in the United States on between ten thousand and twelve thousand standard courses. More courses are being built every day, and about a million or so new players join the ranks each year. The number of driving ranges, putting, and pitch-and-putt courses is inestimable.

There are only three things needed to make a good golfer. They are:

1. Study and application of the simple mechanics of hitting the ball properly.
2. Concentration.
3. Practice.

A standard course plays about seven thousand yards or more, broken up into eighteen units (called holes), numbered consecutively and varying in length from one hundred to as much as (rarely) six hundred yards or more. Play on each hole begins with the players hitting

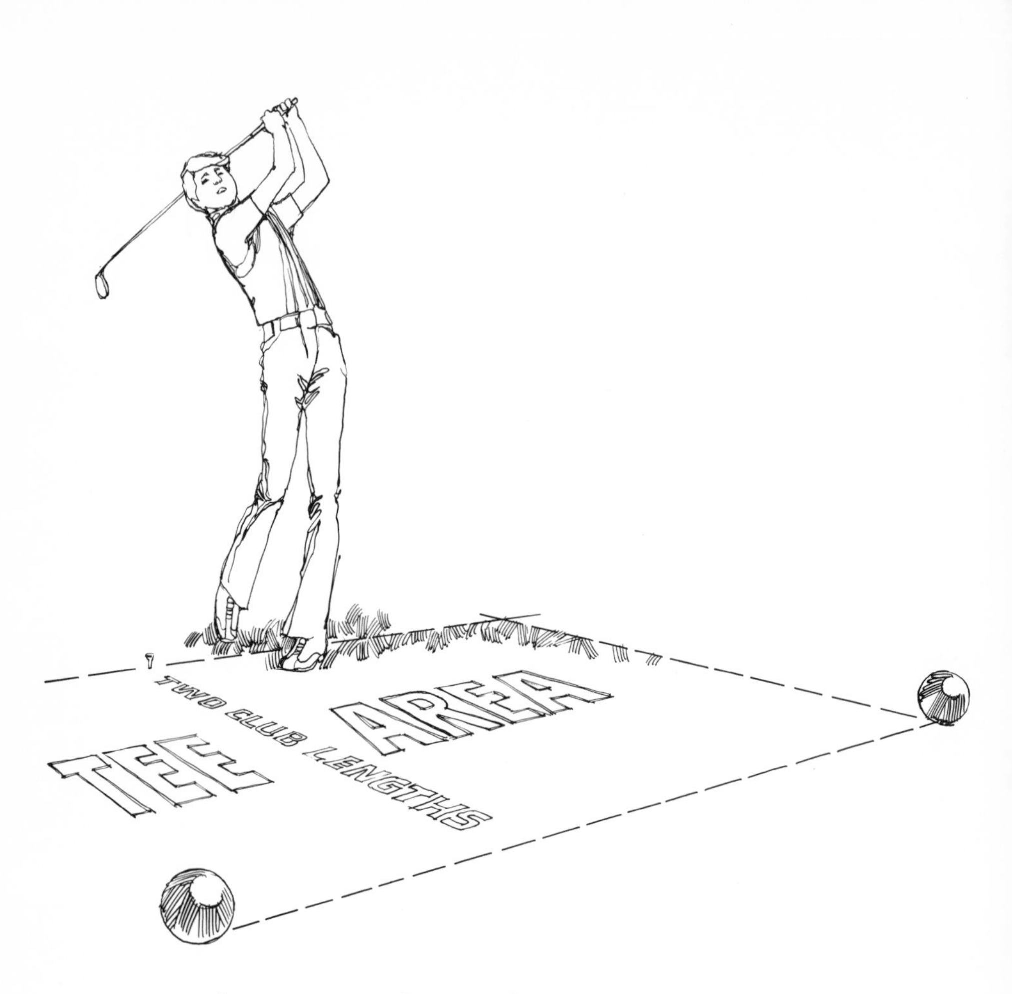

The teeing ground is the only area from which the ball is regularly teed up.

a ball from a small area known as the teeing ground (usually shortened to "the tee") toward an area known as the green, on which is a hole (called the cup) marked by a flag. When the ball is hit into the cup, or "sunk," the player has completed that hole. The object of the game is to hole the ball in the fewest number of strokes.

From the teeing area the ball must be elevated on a small wooden tee or mound of sand to enable a cleaner hit to be made. The teeing ground is the only area from which the ball is regularly teed up. Elsewhere, with a few special exceptions, the ball is played "as it lies."

The green, which surrounds the cup, is a smooth surface of closely cut grass, usually of a variety that has very fine, delicate blades. Sometimes, in places where the special grass will not grow well, the green is of fine sand, packed to allow the ball to roll smoothly.

Between the teeing ground and the green is the fairway, which is covered by coarser grass than is used on the greens, and allowed to grow longer. The fairway usually is bounded by tall grass, trees, and shrubs, known as the rough. The fairway usually is studded with natural or artificial obstacles, such as sand pits (called bunkers or traps), mounds, and water. Such obstacles are called hazards and are located at points best suited to penalize bad shots, thereby increasing the difficulty of scoring well.

The player, or side, entitled to play first from the tee is said to "have the honor." The honor on the first tee is determined by agreement or by the toss of a coin. On subsequent holes the player or side winning a hole takes the honor on the following tee. If a hole has been played even, or "halved," the player or side that had the honor on the preceding tee retains it.

After the balls have been played from the tee, the ball farthest from the hole is played first.

A game is played with a maximum of fourteen hitting instruments, called clubs, which are direct descendants of the bored shepherds' sticks. These clubs are classified as "woods," "irons," and "putters."

Woods, whose hitting surfaces may be made of

wood, plastic, or light metal, are primarily designed for a full stroke to achieve maximum distance from the tee or fairway. Irons are for lofting the ball to intermediate distances, and the putter is for use on the green, where the ball ordinarily is rolled toward the cup and not lofted into the air. Of course, the game may be played with fewer than fourteen clubs, and usually is.

There are two ways of scoring a round: by match play or by stroke (medal) play.

In match play, the side that holes its ball in the fewest number of strokes wins the hole. The side winning the greater number of holes wins the match.

In stroke, (medal) play, the side that takes the fewer number of strokes to complete the match is the winner.

Golf is available to and within the means of just about everyone in the United States. Hardly a locality doesn't have one or more clubs, and most cities have public courses, open to all at comparatively low prices.

The game is remarkably cheap to play in Scotland. At St. Andrews it costs less than three dollars to play eighteen holes, and a full day's play costs only a few cents more.

Driving ranges, where buckets of balls are provided at small cost, and putting and pitch-and-putting courses make it easy to practice without the stress of competition.

CHAPTER TWO

Equipment and Clothes

Since they do most of the work in any well-ordered game, good clubs are essential to good golf.

Today manufacturers turn out masterpieces that are a far cry from the shepherds' crooks that started it all and vastly superior to the instruments with which the Ouimets, Joneses, and Sarazens worked their minor miracles. Clubs in hundreds of designs, within the rigid limitations imposed by the United States Golf Association, are available to meet every individual quirk.

Fewer but better clubs should be the slogan of every beginner; in fact, of every player. Anyone who can make proper use of a driver, putter, and one or two irons can score well. Most players who burden themselves with the allowable full complement of fourteen clubs are either overloading themselves to no avail or doing it strictly for the exercise.

The relative importance and frequency of use of the various clubs may be shown by analyzing an imaginary perfect-par seventy-two over an eighteen-hole course. This would be a round in which not only is par seventy-two scored for the entire eighteen holes, but each hole is played in exactly par figures. On our imaginary course there would be four par five holes, ten par fours, and four par threes (one of which would be 220 yards).

On our perfect-par round, woods certainly would be used fourteen times, from the tee on the par fours and fives. Woods possibly would be employed four more times for second shots on the par fives and perhaps once again from the tee on the long (220-yard) par three. Thus the woods would be used for a minimum of fourteen strokes, possibly nineteen. Since two strokes—no more and no less—are allotted by par to putts on each green for an eighteen-hole total of thirty-six, there would remain only seventeen to twenty-two strokes to be taken care of by all the other iron clubs. The frequency of use of each of the various types of club increases in proportion as higher scores are registered.

From this it becomes apparent that the average player can do well with fewer than the maximum of fourteen clubs. The first officially recognized clubs were only four in number. They were the driver (now also called a No. 1 wood) for distance shots with the ball teed up or from an exceptionally good lie; the brassie (No. 2 wood), with the face only slightly lofted but with a brass plate on the bottom for protection from damage when shooting for distance with the ball not teed up; the baffie (the likes of which no longer exist), which had quite a bit of loft for approach shots to the green, and the putter. All were made of wood and in one piece. It was some years before assembled clubs, some made of metal, were devised.

Equipment and Clothes

It is not necessary to carry many more than the counterparts of the four originals even now. A player who knows how to use them—and stays out of trouble—can do very well on a standard course with a No. 1 wood for use from the tee; a more lofted wood (Nos. 3, 4, or 5) for long shots from the fairway or good lies in the rough; a No. 2 or 3 iron for long shots from bad lies; a No. 5 iron for intermediate distances; a No. 8 or 9 iron for recovery and approach shots, and a putter.

A good set of matched clubs is, of course, an excellent investment, but a beginner who can't buy the full set should buy a few essential clubs of the finest manufacture possible—and build his set from there.

Regardless of how many he buys at the outset, his clubs should all be matched each with the others, a process that reliable manufacturers accomplish with great exactitude. Most matched sets may be purchased piecemeal.

The importance of having clubs matched to each other was conclusively demonstrated when tests were made, after the great champion had retired from competition, of the assortment with which Bobby Jones won everything in sight. All of Jones' clubs were hickory-shafted (he played before metal and plastic shafts had been developed) and were purchased willy-nilly by trial and error. They were not matched by the clubmaker, yet every single one of the clubs Jones finally selected was proved scientifically to be an exact match with the others—except one. The lone wolf in Jones' bag was a club that corresponded to today's No. 8 iron. Jones admitted that particular club had always given him more trouble than the others.

Jones' putter was another story. "Calamity Jane," as the sportswriters and hapless opponents dubbed it, bore no relation to any of the other clubs he carried—or to any other golf instrument known to mankind. A beat-up old piece of junk, it suited Bobby to perfection and played a major role in making him a golfing immortal. It is altogether fitting that Jones carried such an odd-ball putter because the art of holing the ball on the green is highly individualistic and nonconformist. The putter is usually better fitted to whatever style the individual player finds works better for him on the green, rather than being matched in weight, length, balance, etc., to the other clubs in the bag.

In selecting a matched set it usually will be found that if the driver "fits" the player, the other woods and the irons will, too.

If clubs are purchased from one of the more reliable sporting equipment shops or from a Professional Golfers Association shop, the salesman or golf pro can be of great help in making the final selection.

Clubs come in all shaft lengths, and some teaching pros suggest that all players adapt to the more or less conventional forty-three-inch shaft, but it all depends on how the club "feels." If it doesn't feel right, doesn't seem to belong in your hands, feels foreign or awkward in any way, don't buy it—particularly if it is a driver, to which all your other woods and irons should be matched.

As a general rule, drivers with a forty-two-inch shaft are best suited to players below or up to about 5½ feet tall; 42½-inch shafted woods to those from 5½ feet to 5 feet, 7 inches; and 43-inch shafts to those from 5 feet,

7 inches to 6 feet, 1 inch. Drivers are made with shafts up to 50 inches in length for basketball players and the people who always stand in front of you at parades.

The beginner is better off with clubs having fairly flexible shafts. As he improves, and begins to score under a hundred, he may find that medium-flexible shafts will improve his game. Once his scoring begins to hover in the vicinity of par—a point at which the reduction of even one stroke becomes more and more difficult—he may be helped by switching to stiffer shafts.

Being fitted with matched clubs by a concerned and knowledgeable salesman or pro can be quite a ritual—almost as fussy and precise as being measured for a suit of clothes by a tailor in London's Savile Row. And equally rewarding. The well-equipped shop will have an indoor driving range, usually one on which balls are hit to a backstop, and a collection of drivers of all sizes, weights, lengths, and balance. After a customer has been given an eyeball survey for height, weight, length of arms, muscular development, wrists, and other pertinent data, he will be handed a driver that is considered an approximate fit and asked to swing it at a teed-up ball.

From that first swing, no matter how inexperienced and awkward, the knowledgeable salesman can get a pretty good idea of what is called for. A longer or shorter shaft, or a heavier head might be indicated, for instance. When suitable length and weight have been determined, clubs of different balance may be tried. After the salesman has determined the driver he believes suitable in every respect, the final choice still rests with the buyer, of course.

No matter what the testing shows, the driver selected should have the one all-important qualification: It should *feel right* to the one who is going to use it, be almost a natural extension of the arms that are going to swing it in actual play. Exactly what the "right feel" is cannot be explained, but the player will recognize it once he gets his hands on the right club.

Once the purchaser has found his dream driver, the rest is easy. The remaining clubs in a properly matched set will fit the player just as well as the driver does. Sometimes the buyer, just for reassurance, will elect to test a club at the other end of the scale in the matched set—say a No. 8 or 9 iron—to see if it feels as good as the driver. It will, 999 times out of a thousand.

Generally speaking, any club offered for sale by a reputable dealer or a pro shop will be legal under United States Golf Association regulations, but it is handy to know a few restrictions.

The rules say that all parts of any club must be fixed so that the club is one unit; the club cannot be adjustable in any manner. Clubs with interchangeable or adjustable heads, which usually are offered for sale by mail order or novelty shops, are not legal.

A club head, even on the woods, must be longer than it is broad.

All clubs, except putters, must have only one face designed for striking the ball. A putter may have two faces if the loft of both are "substantially the same."

Club faces cannot be concave on the hitting surface, nor can they have any "lines, dots, or other markings with sharp rough edges, or any type of finish for the purpose of unduly influencing the movement of the

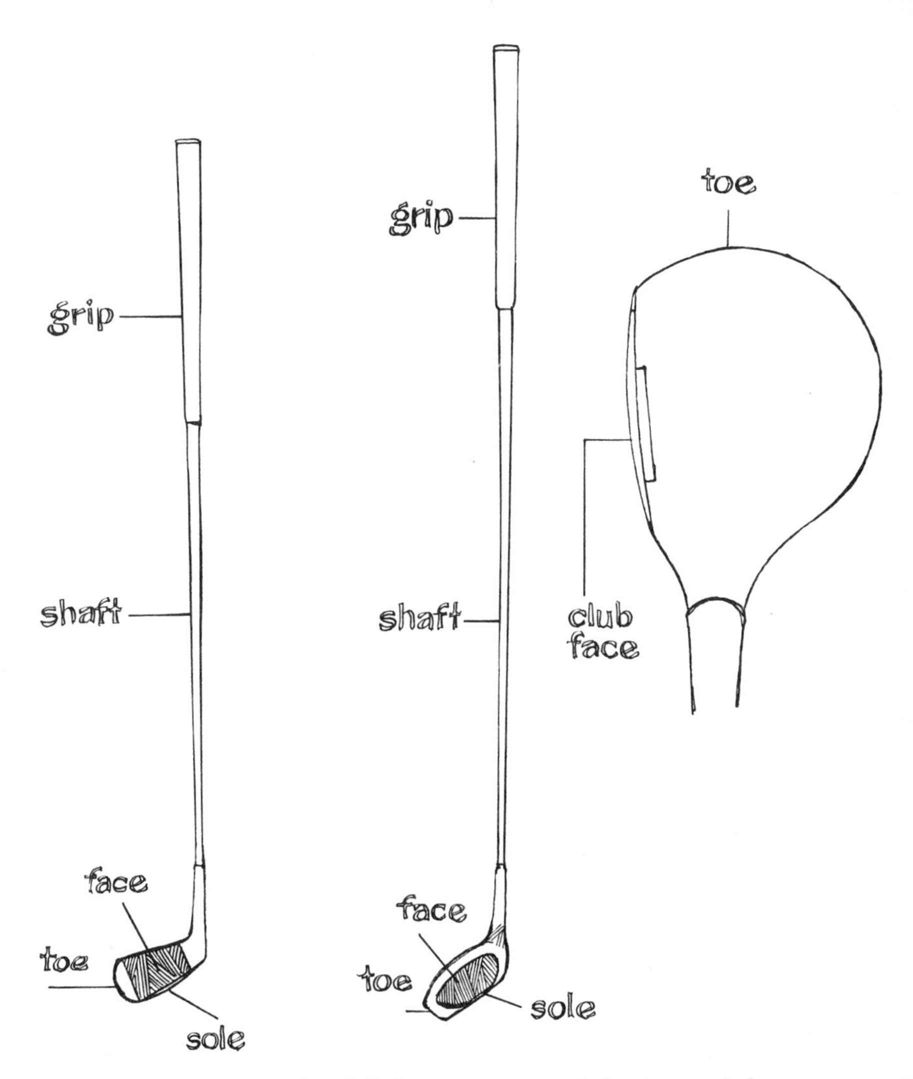

All parts of the club have names, and the faces of the wooden clubs bulge a bit in the middle for more accurate flight.

ball," and the face of an iron club cannot have an inset or attachment. Before these restrictions were imposed by the USGA, irons often were made with all sorts of

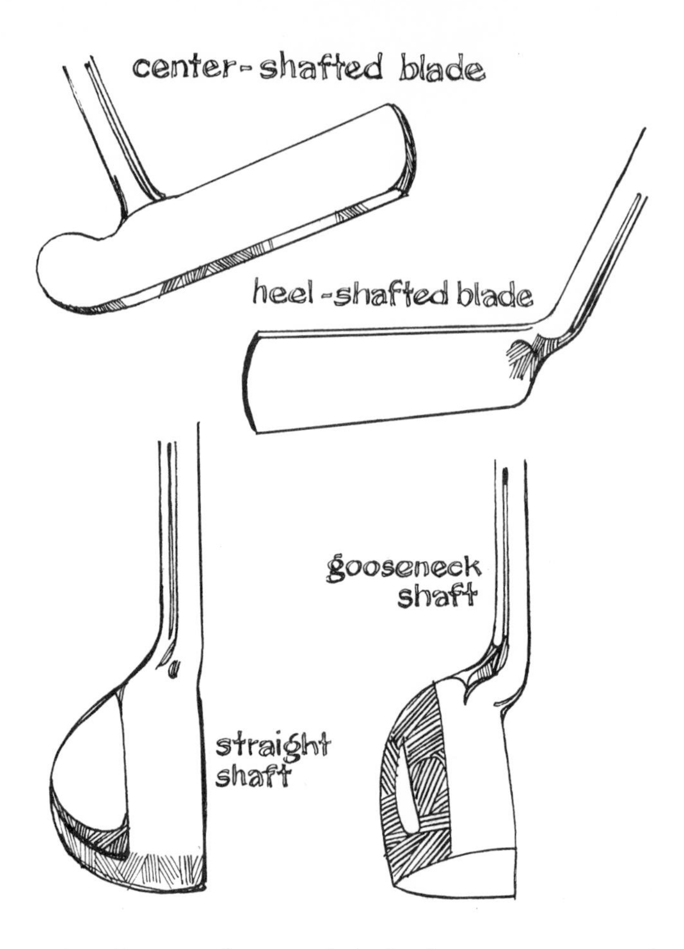

A putter may have a shaft fixed at any point in the head.

faces that imparted backspin, for instance. Backspin is imposed today by skill, not mechanically.

All clubs, except putters, must have a shaft in a straight line with the heel of the club. A putter may have a shaft fixed at any point in the head.

The grip of all clubs must be "substantially straight and plain in form," may have flat sides, but cannot be molded for any part of the hand. The rules say that any device "designed to give the player artificial aid in gripping the club, other than a plain glove" cannot be used, even though it is not part of the club.

A full complement of clubs usually consists of four or five woods, eight or nine irons, and one putter—but no matter how they are scrambled, no more than fourteen may be used during a match.

THE WOODS

The No. 1 wood, the driver, should send the ball anywhere from 175 to 300 yards or more (if you are a Jack Nicklaus or Sam Snead). The head usually is of wood, but may be made of plastic or light metal. The faces of wood clubs bulge a bit in the middle (concave faces are illegal). This is because shots hit slightly toward the outside (or toe) of a wood tend to hook (curve to the left in flight), while those hit toward the inside (heel) may slice (curve to the right in flight). The No. 1 wood is lofted only slightly, just enough to get the ball into the air for a long-distance, low-trajectory flight.

The No. 2 wood once was called a brassie, because it has a brass plate on the bottom (or sole) to protect it from being marred when used from a flat lie. It usually is lofted thirteen or fourteen degrees to compensate for the ball not being teed up when it is used.

At one time there was only one other type of wood, a well-lofted club called a spoon, used for more difficult lies when distance was required. Today, there are three

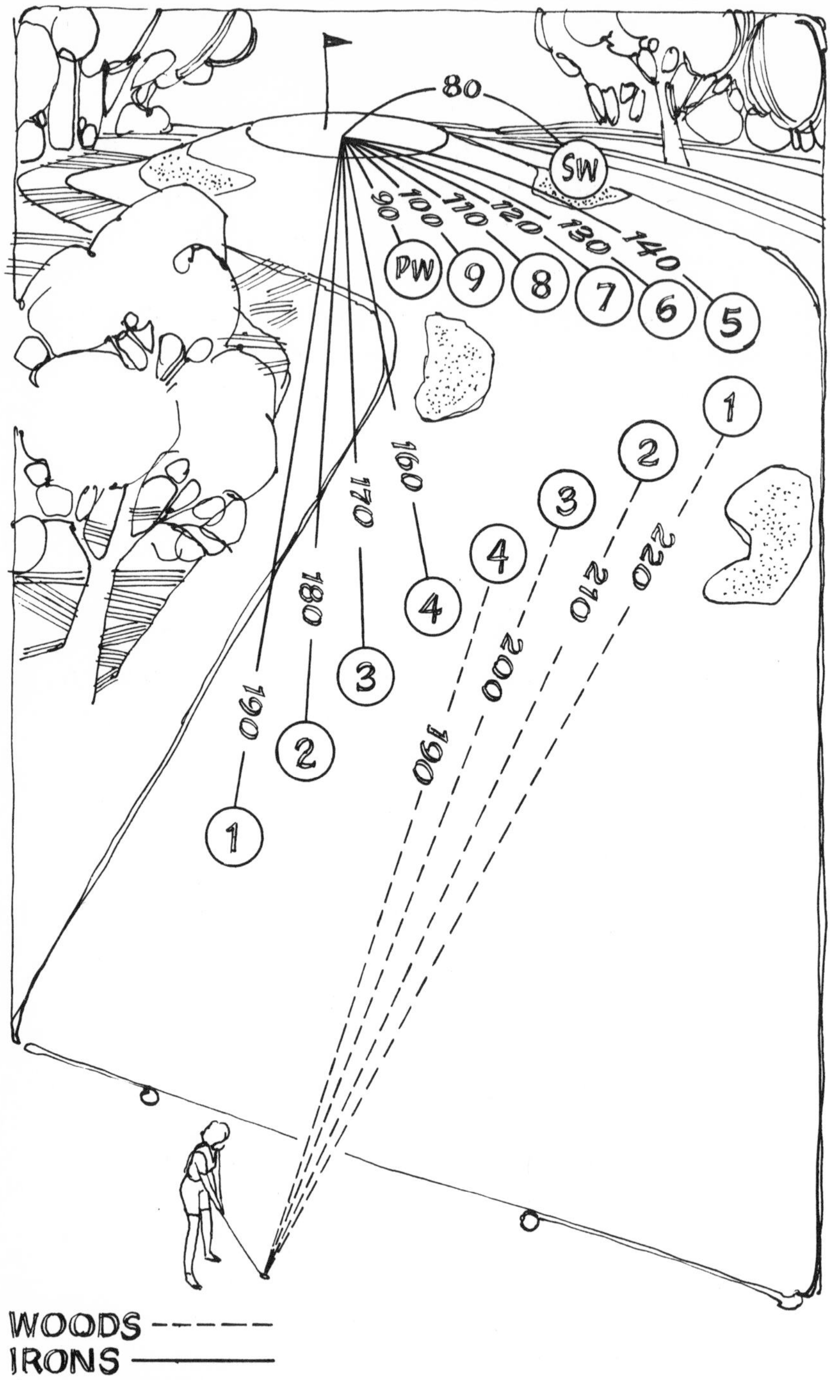

The maximum distances the average golfer can achieve by swinging "well within himself" with the various clubs. The power hitter will do much better.

other woods beside the No. 1 and No. 2. They are the Nos. 3, 4, and 5, whose lofts increase as the number grows larger. They are not only handy for shooting from lies that aren't good enough to permit effective use of the brassie, but for long-distance shots that have to clear high obstacles in their path to the target.

THE IRONS

The regular irons are numbered No. 1 to No. 9, with increased loft of the face from about the same as a driver for the 1 iron to approximately forty-seven de-

Teed-up shots with driver are hit with upward sweep after swing has hit lowest point in arc (left). Fairway woods (Nos. 2, 3, 4, etc.) meet ball at bottom of swing, hitting straight through the ball (left). Don't try to lift the ball; loft of club will tend to that.

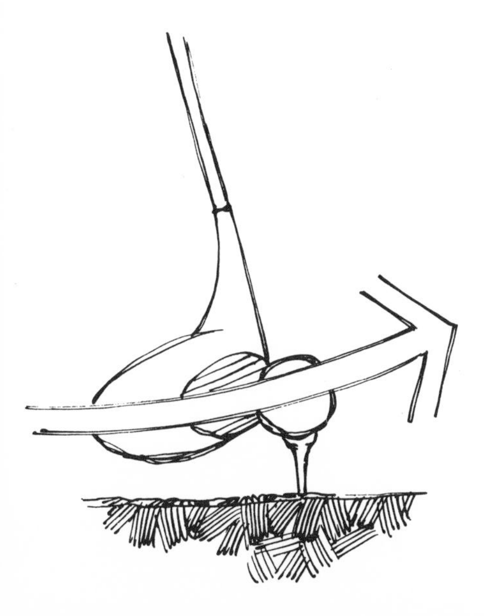

grees for the 9 iron. Naturally, the greater the degree of loft, the higher the flight of the ball and the shorter the distance it will travel. Advanced players can employ the high-numbered irons to apply "backspin," which will stop the ball from rolling once it hits the turf. This is particularly useful in making tight approach shots to greens that do not afford a great deal of room for the ball to roll.

THE WEDGES

The wedges, which were introduced to the game fairly recently by Gene Sarazen, usually are designated pitching wedges (about fifty-one degrees of loft) or sand wedges (fifty-five degrees). Their names pretty well describe the functions they are designed to perform. Early in his career, Sarazen had difficulty shooting out of the sand in traps. He experimented with flanges soldered to the sole of his niblick (9 iron) so the club wouldn't dig into sand or turf as much as most irons with such pronounced loft. He finally hit upon a design that suited him, the USGA approved the principle of the new club, and golfdom had a new and most helpful instrument. Also, it improved Sarazen's game.

THE PUTTER

Books could be and have been written about the putter. Putters are made in a wide variety of design, not only because of the greater latitude permitted by the regulations, but because there just isn't any rigidly prescribed form for putting. On the green it's pretty much every man for himself.

The more commonplace designs are the blade, blade with flange, and mallet types. These may have the shaft anywhere from the heel to the center of the clubhead, and shafts may be either straight or gooseneck (latitude in this respect is also granted by USGA regulations). Even this wide variety is subject to variations. Since at least half the strokes on a round are taken on the green, players have many whims. When a tournament player's game goes sour, it usually is because he isn't putting well. The big playing pros often change putters, sometimes even their putting styles, in an effort at correction.

CLOTHES

Shoes are almost as important to a good game as good clubs. Possibly the best way to play would be barefoot. It is said, perhaps untruthfully, that Sam Snead played without shoes as a boy before he came down from the hills of West Virginia to win the Masters Tournament three times, the PGA three times, and the British Open once, but this would be considered eccentric in better golfing circles today.

Ordinary leather just doesn't give the firm grip to the ground that is so necessary to good shots. Rubber and composition soles, no matter how they are rippled or corrugated, tend to slip on wet turf. The best golf shoes yet devised are studded with specially designed spikes.

blade
(standard)
blade
(with flange)
mallet

Equipment and Clothes

Other clothing should allow freedom of movement. Great freedom in color and design is permissible, but outlandish getups should be avoided. A player should attract attention on the course only by the way he plays, not because he looks like a freak.

CHAPTER THREE

Getting Ready

Getting ready to hit a golf ball is almost as important as the swing itself. Unless you grip the club properly and your address (the way you stand) is as it should be, the whole thing will get off on the wrong foot.

The golf swing actually begins when you pick up the club you are going to use. You must hold it properly if you are to make any kind of shot at all.

The grip is to the golf swing as rudder controls are to a ship. If the rudder is wobbly because its connections with the ship's steering wheel are sloppy and loose, no amount of spinning of the wheel can keep the craft on a steady, true course.

The hands are the only contact a golfer has with the club, and if his grip is basically unsound or sloppy he cannot keep control of the club and bring the face of the club into contact with the ball smartly and decisively as he should, except occasionally by happenstance.

Getting Ready

The player must grip the club not only in a manner that gives tight, but not tense, control, but so that his hands act as a single unit throughout the swing. That is why the so-called "baseball grip," in which each hand grips the club independently, generally does not work too well. True, a few successful golfers have used it, but they are in an underwhelming minority. Bob Rosburg, a leading touring pro, has used it effectively to win many championships and set several records, but he is exceptional in many respects. He doesn't even believe in practicing—"a little putting, that's all."

The most widely used grip was conceived by Harry Vardon around the turn of the century. Naturally, it was dubbed the Vardon grip. Before Vardon had his brainstorm, which enabled the hands to take united action, players used the ancient St. Andrews, or two-handed baseball grip.

In the Vardon grip, the hands are united to work together by overlapping each other. In a variation, called the interlocking grip, unison of the hands is achieved by intertwining fingers.

The overlapping is by far the most widely used of all grips. To achieve it, lay a club in your left hand with an inch or so of the butt end of the shaft extending beyond the palm (Figure 1). The grip of the club should extend from a point at the middle joint of the index finger at the bottom to just below the little finger toward the butt.

Close the left hand with the thumb extending down the leather toward the side of the shaft opposite the direction of flight. The back of the hand should point toward the line of flight, with the first two or three knuckles showing to the player. The V formed by the thumb and index finger should point to the right shoulder (Figure 2). Pressure should be felt on the little, ring, and index fingers. This pressure should be maintained firmly, but not tensely, throughout the swing. Losing control with these fingers at any point (usually at the top of the swing) can cause your grip, and consequently your swing, to disintegrate—with disastrous results.

Once the left hand is closed, place the club in the fingers of the right hand (Figure 3). It will be noted that the right-hand grip is entirely in the fingers. Close the right hand with the palm facing toward the line of flight and the little finger of the right hand overlapping the index finger of the left hand. The thumb of the right hand should be resting against the right index finger. The V formed by the index finger and the thumb of the right hand also should point toward the right shoulder (Figure 4).

In the variation of the Vardon known as the interlocking grip, the little finger of the right hand is entwined with the index finger of the left hand, instead of overlapping it.

The Vardon grip may seem unnatural at first, especially when contrasted to the more instinctive baseball grip, in which each hand grasps the club separately. In time you will become accustomed to the Vardon grip, will get the feel of it, and realize how sweet it is to have the hands united throughout the swing.

Now comes a very important step in preparing yourself to play golf properly. It is a process you will repeat many times before you become a good golfer.

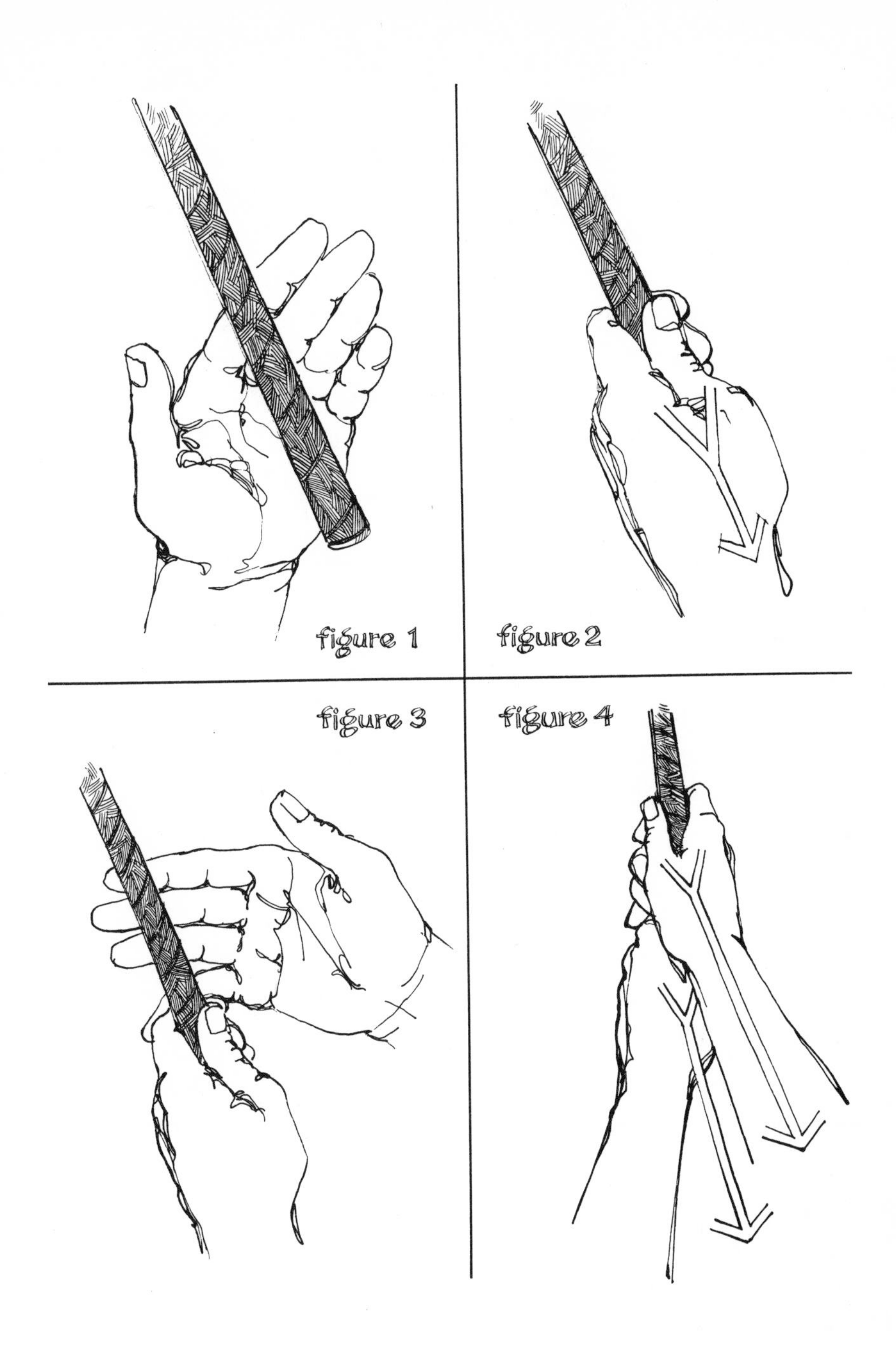
figure 1
figure 2
figure 3
figure 4

You must practice your grip until it becomes completely natural, until you *hold the club properly with both hands without giving it a thought.* Pick up a club the right way every chance you get. Check your grip at all points to make sure that it is absolutely correct. After you have done this often enough you will find that you take the proper grip naturally—subconsciously, as it were. When the proper grip becomes second nature—as natural as shaking hands or picking up a pen to write or any of the countless other things you do repeatedly without conscious effort—you have laid the groundwork for an excellent game.

Whether to adopt the overlapping or interlocking grip is a matter of personal preference, but the weight of evidence points to the overlapping as being the more efficient. Almost without exception the great professionals use it, as do an overwhelming majority of the better amateurs.

The interlocking grip is sometimes recommended for players with small hands, but here a warning: If the fingers are weak, the interlocking grip can throw too much strain on them, resulting in loss of control of the club.

It is suggested that the novice start with the overlapping grip and, after his game has progressed, monkey around with the interlocking grip if he feels it can improve his game. Chances are that he will be happy with the overlapping grip.

The next step in preparing to hit the ball is the address, the position taken by a player before beginning a stroke. It is as important as any other phase of the game. If the player's feet and posture are not as they should be, the golf shot cannot be made properly. It is highly important to get off to a good start.

The launching pad for every stroke in golf is the stance: the position of the feet when addressing the ball.

There are three stances used for conditions ordinarily encountered in the game. They are:

1. Square Stance, sometimes called the accuracy stance because it tends to aid accuracy in placement of shots. The feet are even with the intended line of flight and are closer together than in the closed stance. This stance is used mostly for the medium irons (Nos. 4, 5, and 6).

2. Closed Stance, for power. The feet are placed approximately shoulder width apart and the right foot is drawn back from the intended line of flight by two or three inches. This is generally employed with the woods and long-distance irons (Nos. 1, 2, and 3).

3. Open Stance, which is especially helpful when backspin is desired. The feet are closer together than in either of the other stances, and the left foot is drawn back two or three inches from the intended line of flight. This stance is mostly used with the high-arc, short-distance clubs, such as the Nos. 7, 8, and 9 irons and the wedges.

It is suggested that the beginner indicate the line of intended flight of the ball with a club or some other marker to which he can adjust his feet in assuming the proper stance.

The posture of the body is the next important adjustment to be made in addressing the ball. All good golfers "sit down to the ball," as they express it. This means that their knees are not locked but are slightly flexed. The amount of knee bend should not be exaggerated, but just enough to allow freedom of the body throughout the swing. This is something to which you can adjust yourself (within limitations) to your liking as you go through your "training practice" swings.

Most good golfers turn their toes slightly out in the stance, but this too is a matter of adjustment, which you will make as you go along. Generally speaking, the feet in the stance should be as they are when you walk, unless, of course, you are terribly pigeon-toed or walk with your toes pointed way out. The main object in the stance is to feel comfortable and as though you belonged in the position of the stance.

At the address, the body should be bent forward from the waist at not more than a thirty-to-thirty-five-degree angle. A completely upright position is undesirable because it results in the shoulders turning too much on the horizontal and otherwise messes up the swing.

On the other hand, bending too far forward from the waist causes the sole of the club to tilt and not rest flat on the ground, as it should.

To sum up, at address you should look exactly as though you were just starting to sit down: knees flexed, body bent forward slightly from the waist, rear end sticking out a bit. This explains the term "sitting down to the ball."

After assuming your stance, place the ball on a line just about even with your left heel, so that your head at address will be slightly behind the target point.

Many novices are unduly concerned over how far to

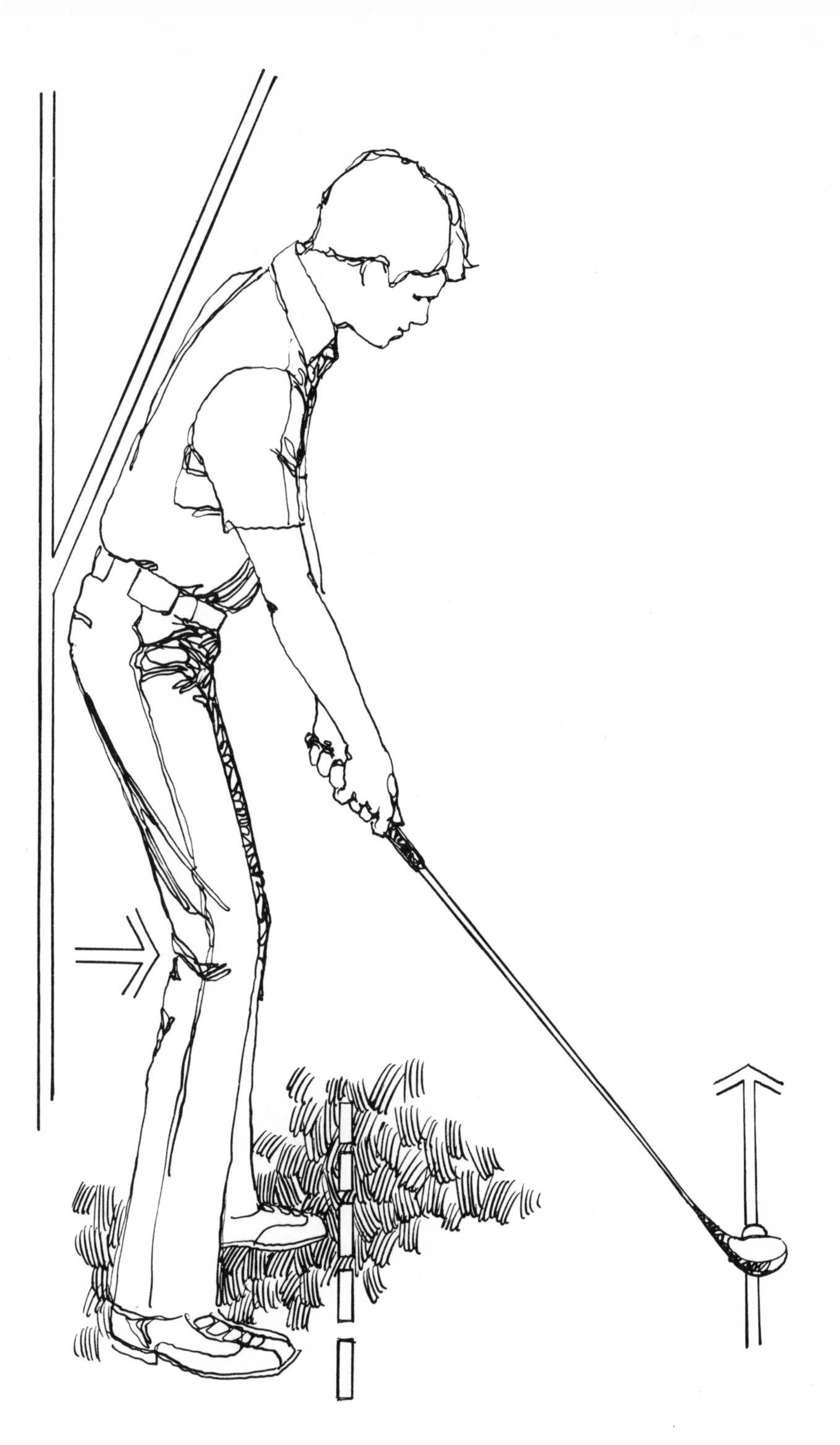

At address, player is "sitting down to the ball" (note knees slightly flexed, not locked), body bent forward from the waist, arms extending naturally toward the ball, not reaching.

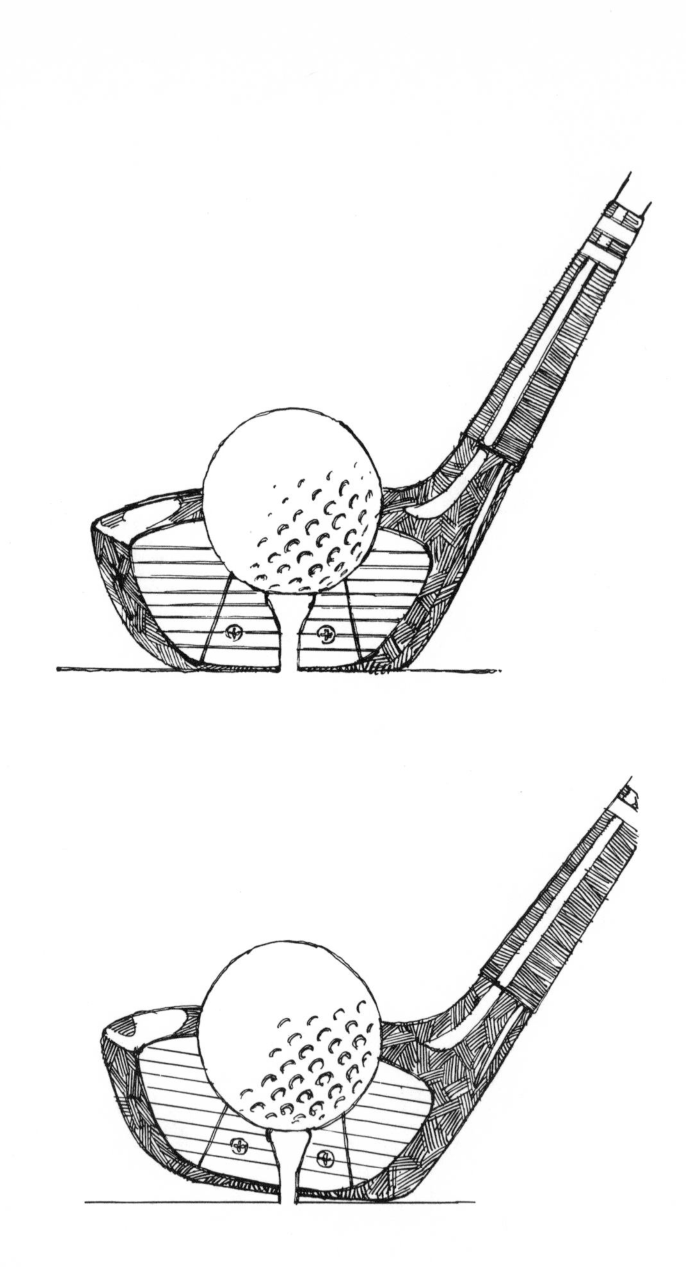

Sole of the driver should rest flat on ground (above), not tilted (below).

stand from the ball at address so that it may be hit squarely. This is an easy problem. You simply tee up the ball so that about half of it shows above the club's face. Then take the driver in your left hand—with the proper grip, of course—with your right hand dangling at your side. Then adjust your feet so that when you have assumed the proper stance *the sole of the club rests flat on the ground* and the face of the club is squarely behind the ball. When you have settled comfortably in this position, complete the grip with the right hand—and you are in proper position. The arms should neither reach for the ball so that they are straight out, nor should they be pulled too close to the body so that your position is cramped.

Practice the address until it too, like the grip, has become second nature. During the "conditioning" period, check each point—the stance, the body bend, the knee flex—until taking the right position at address becomes second nature, just as the grip has.

You are now ready to hit the ball, but the best advice that can be given at this point is: DON'T!

CHAPTER FOUR

The Big Swing

Once you have addressed the ball properly you are in position to hit it, but as we said before, DON'T! That is, not seriously.

If you want to see just how far you are from being able to play golf, you might take a swing at the ball. If you do, the chances are ten to one that you will miss the ball completely on the first try. If you don't whiff, the odds are fifty to one that the ball won't go where you aimed it, won't even take off for a long flight, but will dribble feebly from the tee or hop merrily along the ground for a few yards like a ruptured rabbit. Or it may take off in a high arc and land almost where it started from. If you do hit the ball solidly, it probably will slice or hook like a boomerang. In other words, the ball will go almost anywhere but where you want it to.

If, perchance, against a thousand-to-one odds, you should hit a long ball that flies straight and lands somewhere near where you wanted it to go, try again. If the second ball you hit also performs creditably and the third, you probably are that one in a hundred thousand who has a perfect or near perfect natural swing.

Either that, or your coordination and reflexes are so amazing that you can get fairly good results with almost any old kind of swing. In that case, you should apply yourself with extra diligence to learning good form because you can become one of the immortals, the big winners.

To avoid embarrassment and discouragement and to achieve a really fine game, devote your efforts from the beginning to perfecting your swing before you ever take a serious swipe at a real, live ball. *The importance of this cannot be overemphasized.*

The one big difference between a good golfer and a bad golfer is that the good golfer has practiced the proper swing until it has become so automatic that *he does not give it a thought while he is in the process of hitting the ball.* The only thing a good golfer thinks about during his swing is hitting the ball properly to go where he wants it to. If a golfer's mind wanders during his swing from intense concentration on *hitting the ball,* to wonder if his grip is firm, his body weight shifting properly, or any of the other components of a good swing, he is dead. That is the main reason it is advisable for the beginner to *practice* his swing until it has become automatic before playing or even making a serious pass at a ball. When a good swing becomes almost a reflex action, it is time to take to the course, and not before.

It is best to begin to learn how to play with the full swing of the drive because this is the one basic swing in golf. *Everything you will need to score well from tee to green is in the big swing.* Putting, of course, is a different art.

Players of different builds do not need different swings, nor does a player need a different swing for different clubs. There is a natural variation in swinging different clubs, but it is not made consciously; it is caused by the difference in address and the difference in clubs used.

As an example, you stand farthest from the ball when using a driver because the ball is teed up, the shaft is longer, and the sole of the club (which must be flat at address) is at a flatter angle to the shaft than with other clubs. As the clubs you use grow shorter, you move closer to the ball and play the ball from a position more toward your right foot. This causes you automatically to take a more upright posture, and results in a naturally shorter swing. This is done automatically and not by conscious adjustment.

Although the full swing should be so fluid that it seems one motion, we shall learn it in two parts, then put them together.

THE BACKSWING

Check your stance (square or slightly closed) and position of the practice ball, or whatever you are using as a target (in line with your left heel). Check your posture (body slightly bent forward from waist, rear end protruding, knees flexed, weight on left foot). Make sure the sole of the driver's face is square to the ball, or simulated ball, and its sole is flat on the ground. Check your grip and make sure most of your weight is on the left foot.

The Big Swing

After you have run through your checklist, give the club head what golfers call a waggle, or two or three. You waggle by waving the club head over the ball by loosely swinging your wrists. The waggle is supposed to eliminate tension, make you feel at home with the club in motion, and help establish the rhythm of the swing. Whether it accomplishes all these things or not is a moot point, but good golfers employ the waggle, so it must have some benefit.

If it serves any purpose at all, the waggle loosens up the player for the drive. It is like revving the motor a time or two before setting an automobile in motion. The forward press—a movement that is scarcely noticeable in many of the better players—is the actual start of the big swing.

Place the club head down behind the ball, which should be teed up so that about half of it is above the club's face, or hitting surface. Then move the right knee (still flexed) in toward the left knee an inch or two, without shifting the weight from the left foot. This automatically brings the hands slightly ahead of the ball. Then return the right knee to its original position. The hands and arms have not only pressed forward, but upon return to the original position you have actually started the backswing.

Continue the motion started by the forward press, bringing the club head back low and slow from the ball. Speed is not essential at this point; the main idea is to get the big swing under way rhythmically, smoothly, and in the right orbit.

The left arm—which should be straight but not rigid—dominates this movement, but the right arm should

work with it in perfect coordination. The start of the backswing should be parallel to the ground for anywhere between a foot or eighteen inches. In this phase of the big swing, the club head should not *drag* on the ground, but should *swing* straight back an inch or two off the ground.

If the club head is lifted abruptly from the ball, the entire swing will be off to a bad start; it will tend to become jerky and lose its rhythm and fluid flow throughout. An abrupt takeaway also causes the wrists to cock too quickly, with resultant loss of control.

After the club head is lifted into the circular swing, the wrists will cock themselves automatically when the hands are about waist high if the left arm remains straight.

Perhaps now is a good time to explain about the straight left arm, which should prevail throughout the big swing. The left arm should be kept as straight as possible, but never locked rigidly. Throughout the swing the left arm should be as though it were an extension of the club shaft, communicating to the shoulders.

The "left arm straight" business has been a bugaboo to golfers since the days of Bobby Jones. Jones' physique enabled him to keep a perfectly straight left arm throughout without any strain, so the pundits ruled that all golfers should do the same. Some just cannot, and their efforts have resulted in some hideous and catastrophic big swings. The left arm should be kept as straight as possible, but not rigid. It is probable that in the beginning you will not be able to complete the full backswing—with the club shaft horizontal—and do this.

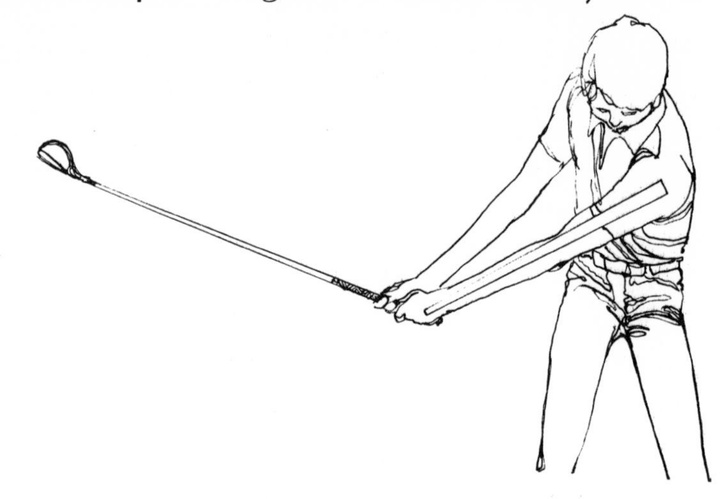

Usually as the swing is practiced, the muscles loosen up, and by the time you are actually ready to employ the big swing in hitting a ball, you will be able to achieve the full backswing with a straight, but not locked, left arm. Some of the better tournament players never do achieve the full backswing. They bring the club back so that the shaft is short of being horizontal. They achieve good results, or they wouldn't be tournament players, but the very best comes only from a full backswing.

The right elbow should be kept as close to the body as is comfortable during the backswing, but it can float away to enable the player to keep his left arm straight. Jack Nicklaus, for instance, floats his right elbow way out into outer space at the top of his swing, but his superb coordination and timing enable him to get it back in place—close to his body—in time for his tremendous impact with the ball, in which he exerts power from his hands, arms, shoulders, body, and legs.

The Big Swing

During the backswing, the arms, hips, and shoulders act as one unit. The body turns, but it doesn't sway; head and shoulders remain directly over the ball. The shoulders rotate—but don't sway—so that the left shoulder dips under the chin, pointing at the ball. The hips move as though you were trying to turn around without moving your feet. The weight automatically shifts from the left foot to the right, which should be bearing practically all the weight at the top of the backswing.

Shifting of weight causes the left knee to point toward the ball at top of backswing, foot rolling inside.

This shifting of weight will cause the left knee to point toward the ball at the top of the swing, with the left foot rolling to the inside, perhaps the heel lifted.

At the top of the backswing, the sole of the club should be pointing toward the intended line of flight of the ball, and the face of the club head should be square with the line of flight, not "shut" (pointing toward the sky) or "open" (pointing toward the ground). As we said before, at the top of the backswing, the left shoulder should point directly at the ball.

The grip should remain firm, but not tense, throughout the backswing. At the top of the backswing the thumb of the left hand should be under the shaft.

There are three checkpoints in the backswing, points at which, during the period you are perfecting the big swing, you can stop and check to see that you are doing things properly.

1. When the club head has been taken one foot to eighteen inches back from the ball, low and straight, just before the swing begins to "pick it up." At this point your left arm should be straight, your hands about even with your right leg. Your left shoulder should be just beginning to dip toward the ball, and your weight should be starting to shift from your left foot to your right. Your head may start to rotate, but must never change its position of being directly over the ball. Your hips will already have started to swivel as your left knee begins to point toward the ball.

2. About halfway through the backswing, when your hands are about waist high. The left shoulder should

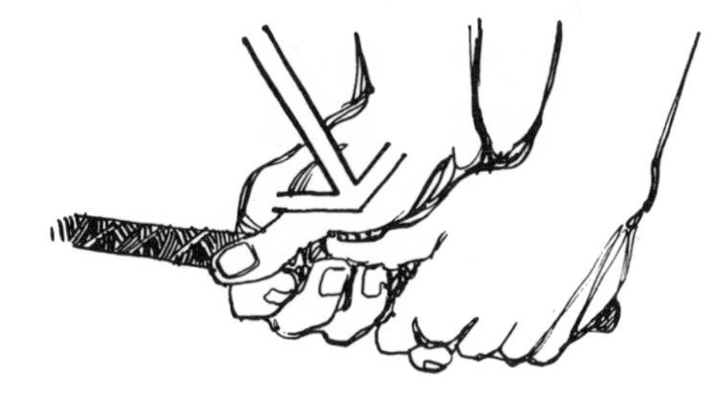

At top of backswing, left thumb should be under shaft.

be well on its way to a point directly under the chin, the hands just beginning to cock, and the weight slightly on the right foot. The waist will have turned, which comes about naturally if the backswing movement has been centered around the shoulders, which serve the same function as the hub in a turning wheel.

3. At the top of the backswing, check to make certain that the face of the club is square to the line of flight, sole pointing toward the target. Be certain that the hands have not lost control of the club and that the grip is still firm but not tense. The left thumb should be under the club shaft. The left shoulder should be under the chin, hips should have turned so that the left knee is pointing toward the ball. At this point, weight should be squarely on the right foot, with the left acting as a balance, rather than as a weight carrier.

One of the most important things to remember in the big swing—or any golf swing—is *don't move your head.* If the shoulders are the hub of the swing, the head is the axle. The head can rotate, but it must stay

At top of backswing, face of club should be square to line of flight, sole pointing toward target. Left shoulder should be under chin, hips turned so that left knee points to ball.

in a fixed position with regard to the ball. It should not move backward or forward or bob up and down. If the head sways, it indicates that you are not pivoting properly, the top of your body is not remaining over the ball. This can be disastrous.

The Big Swing

If your head bobs up and down, it means that your shoulders are not rotating around it and you won't come up with your left shoulder tucked under your chin and pointing at the ball, as it should.

With most good golfers, the backswing is noticeably slower than the downswing, during which the power is applied. Some good golfers, however, do have fast backswings. This is something you can adjust to your liking after you have put the big swing all together in one piece.

Practice the backswing, with frequent stops at checkpoints to see that you are doing everything right, until it too—like the grip—has become an almost reflex action.

Then you will be ready for the downswing.

The big backswing.

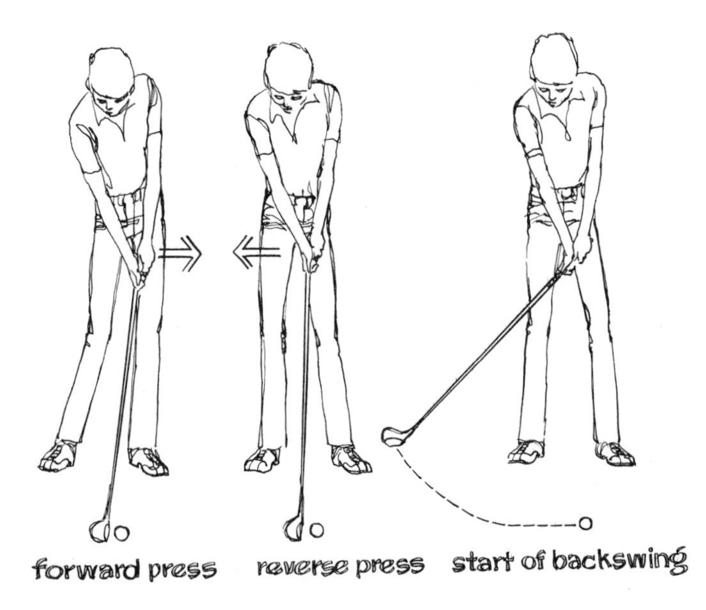

The big downswing.

THE DOWNSWING

Practically all good golfers pause at the top of the backswing before reversing the path of the club into the downswing. With some the pause is so brief as to be virtually imperceptible. In others it is quite noticeable. This, too, is something you will have to adjust to your liking once you have assembled the complete big swing. Whatever gives you the best sense of unbroken rhythm and smoothness in the full big swing is the best for you.

There is disagreement, even among the best of golfers, as to how the club should be started in the downswing. Some say the downswing should be started by pulling the left arm down. Others insist that the downswing should be triggered by turning the hips slightly toward the left in their reverse pivot.

Whatever the answer, it is a fact that in a well-hit drive the hips are ahead of the club at the moment of impact. Study of hundreds of slow-motion and stop-action motion pictures has convinced me that most of the better golfers start the downswing with the hips, closely followed by the arm action. This also eliminates most of the danger of the club head getting ahead of the hips at the moment of impact.

So, for the time being, it is suggested that the downswing be started with the hips moving in their reverse pivot just a split second ahead of the arms or by beginning to shift your weight from the right foot to the left (where it winds up on the follow-through).

The right elbow should return to your side naturally without interrupting the smooth flow of the swing and without bending the left arm.

The wrists will uncock automatically as they pass your belt line and enter the hitting area.

The right foot digs in to help speed up the club head as you enter the hitting area, which is approximately two-thirds through the downswing, when the hands are about waist high, and they begin to uncock to add the last bit of power to the club head.

Impact should be against a firm left side and at the precise moment when the club head attains maximum speed.

During the downswing, as throughout the big swing, the hands should maintain a firm but not rigid grip,

The right arm returns to the right side and the wrists uncock automatically as the club head enters the hitting area.

holding the club in its appointed path firmly.

At the moment of impact, the weight is on the left foot, with the right foot digging in to add speed to the club's movement. The left arm and the club's shaft should form an almost straight line. The arms should be working in unison to achieve maximum speed of the club head. The right shoulder should be well down, and the head should have remained in the same relative position to the ball as it was at address.

There are several points during the downswing at which action may be stopped and positions are checked during practice.

One is when the hands are a bit less than shoulder high. At this point the wrists should still be cocked, the left arm—still straight, but not rigid—should be

In the downswing, weight shifts to left foot, and right foot digs in to add speed to club's movement.

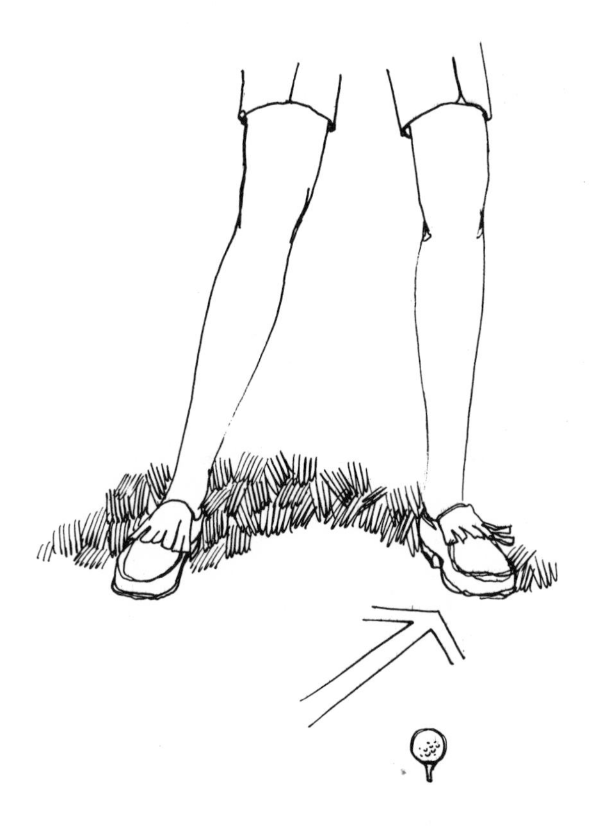

When hands are a bit less than shoulder high, wrists should still be cocked and the left arm straight, but not rigid. The left hip should have moved well out of the way.

parallel to the ground, the left hip should have moved well out of the way of the swing, and weight distribution should be about even between the left and right feet.

When the hands are about waist high they should begin to uncock to add their power to the impact. The left shoulder should be in an almost normal position, and the right elbow should have returned close to the right side. Check again to make certain that the head has not wobbled from side to side or bounced up and down. Remember, it can rotate with the shoulder, but must never vary position in relation to the ball, that is, sway from side to side or bob up and down.

The moment of impact is the time to remember one very essential thing: *Keep your head down.* More good shots have been ruined by lifting the head than perhaps any other mistake. This is caused by a natural eagerness to see where the ball has gone, how effective the stroke has been. Usually, the head is lifted a split second *before* the ball has been hit, thus completely spoiling the firm, square contact so essential to a good shot. The head must remain down, eyes glued on the spot where the ball *was* until the natural flow of the follow-through brings the eyes to a level where they can follow the flight of the ball. Even if this takes a full second or two, the ball will still be in flight and plainly visible when the eyes have been refocused to bring it into clear view. The importance of keeping the head down cannot be overemphasized. It is essential to all good shot-making, even in putting.

This brings us to the last, but by no means least, phase of the big swing: the follow-through.

THE FOLLOW-THROUGH

There should be no conscious effort to stop the big swing once the ball has been hit. The swing will just die naturally after the right knee and shoulder have passed under the head—which must still be in a fixed position. The club head travels out as the right hip rolls through the shot. Now, and now only, may the straight—or fairly straight—left arm be bent. Some good golfers wind up with both arms seemingly wrapped around their heads. Others keep the arms fairly straight and finish with their hands fairly high. A good follow-through, following a good downswing and accurate impact, will pull the right heel off the ground. It is most important that the left side has not swayed during the impact and after. It should remain vertical.

CHAPTER FIVE

Putting It All Together

Although every game of golf has thrilling moments, there is nothing more exciting or inspiring than a well-hit drive from the tee.

The drive is the beginning of every hole in a round except the three or four par threes on a standard course, and nothing gives so much confidence for the task that lies ahead as a ball hit long and straight down the fairway from the tee.

It is a fact that not all drivers who hit a long ball—or even a long, straight ball—are necessarily players who score well. It is also a fact that all golfers who score well consistently hit fairly long and certainly accurately placed shots with their woods.

H. B. Fairnie wasn't very well known as a golfer, but he did gain a measure of fame as a golf writer. Under the pseudonym "A Keen Hand," in 1857 he had published in England what is generally believed to be the first book on golf. *The Golfer's Manual* may be outdated as an instruction book, but Fairnie's philosophy of the game never will be.

"Long driving, if it be not the most deadly, is certainly the most dashing and fascinating part of the game," he wrote, "and of all others the principal difficulty of Golfers to acquire; and his chief delight when he can manage it."

So putting the big swing together to achieve the long, straight drive can be one of the most rewarding efforts in golf, and, since the big swing is the basic swing of all golf (with the possible exception of putting), the most important.

It is perfectly natural to be impatient to get out on the course to see how well you can do, but remember: *For every moment you spend at swinging practice and getting the big swing together, you will receive hours of reward once you actually have started to play the game.*

It is far better to iron out the wrinkles in your swing at this point than to practice *mistakes* in actual play, or suffer from indecision and the shattering of concentration that comes from not doing everything in the big swing easily and without conscious thought about details.

The purpose of preplay practice is to make the big swing as natural to you as walking or running or sitting down or any of the other things you do every day without giving a conscious thought to *how* you do them. When you have accomplished that, you can take your place on the golf course without fear of looking ridiculous and with full confidence that you probably are a better player than most who have been playing golf for a long time.

In putting the big swing together, you should

achieve the feeling that you are applying centrifugal force, as when a weight is swung in a circle at the end of a cord.

Some instructors use a unique club to impart the centrifugal force, "weight on a cord" feeling to the beginner. The bottom portion of the club is a length of chain to which is attached an iron ball, slightly heavier than the head of a driver. When this club is swung properly, the chain straightens out until it is as straight as the shaft, and the "feel" of the proper swing is imparted to the student golfer. Of course, this club cannot be used for practicing a full swing (the chain portion would sag at the top of the backswing), nor is it used to hit a ball, but it serves its designated purpose very well.

In the truly coordinated and rhythmic swing there is no strain. It is a true swing, with no levering action. We have all seen flywheels, which travel their arcs at tremendous speeds without any outward signs of the power they are exerting—as long as the wheel is symmetrical and well constructed. That is centrifugal force at its best. That is what you must achieve in the big swing to hit the ball long and straight.

Failure to achieve the "weight on a cord" feel explains why so many golfers strain and labor, only to produce bad drives. Most dubs never feel the carefree, dynamic sensation that comes from hitting the ball with a truly centrifugal force swing. They don't know what a pleasure they are missing.

So if you want to step out on the course for your first regular round feeling confident and qualified to hold your own with more experienced players—or even excel them—practice the big swing until it has become second nature, until you do it almost automatically without giving a thought to the nitty-gritty details.

During the practice swings, before you take to the driving range or golf course, you can still think about the things you must do to make a perfect big swing, since you won't have to concentrate on hitting a ball.

Bear in mind that the essential elements in the big swing are:

Proper stance and address, which sets the stage.
Shifting of the weight.
The pivot or body turn.
Club control through the hands throughout.
The follow-through.

At address, in the slightly "sitting down" position, the weight should be slightly back on the heels and evenly distributed on the inside of each foot. For balance, weight should *not* be on the balls of the feet, as though you were getting ready to take off on a sprint.

About 75 or 80 percent of the weight shifts to the right foot on the backswing and the left foot rolls over toward the inside, or the left heel may be raised slightly, whichever feels most comfortable. The left heel, if raised at all, should be elevated only slightly. Raising it several inches tends to pull the head and body away from the ball.

The club head should be brought back on a straight line for a foot or so, low to the ground but not dragging.

Putting It All Together

The left arm should remain as straight as you can comfortably keep it throughout the backswing, so that the club becomes practically an extension of the left arm. Keeping the left arm as straight as possible gives a wider, and consequently more powerful, arc to the swing. Bending the left arm too much not only ruins the arc of the swing, it creates an awkward position at the top of the backswing.

Of course, the right elbow must leave the body if the left arm is to be kept reasonably straight, but do not let it drift any farther out than is necessary.

Never forget that the backswing should be a turn, not a sway; the head and upper body should remain directly over the ball, or whatever you are aiming at in practice. The proper pivot action is made exactly as though you were turning around to look at someone behind you. The hips and shoulders turn in coordinated unison, and the left shoulder should automatically tilt until it is under the chin at the top of the backswing.

Don't "lose the club" at the top of the swing. The last three fingers of the left hand particularly must maintain a firm, but not tense, grip throughout the swing, but particularly at the top of the swing.

Whether to pause perceptibly at the top of the backswing is entirely up to you. Some do, some don't. Do whatever feels best, but remember: *The good golfer never starts his downswing until the backswing is finished.* If you have to pause to do this, then pause.

On the downswing the left knee becomes straight as the hips and shoulders turn to the left. Everything in the downswing adds up to a transfer of weight mainly to the left side, so that you will be hitting against a firm left side. As the weight flows smoothly to the left side, the left foot rolls back to its original position. Simultaneously, the right foot rolls over to the inside, and its heel may start leaving the ground just at impact.

The right elbow should start returning to the right side early in the downswing. This helps the right shoulder to lower as it should in the downswing. It also helps to keep the club from cutting across the ball from the outside, which imparts that most familiar of all sights on a golf course: the slice.

Remember to keep your head down and your eyes fixed on whatever you are using as a practice target. The head should be kept down, even in the follow-through. Lifting the head in anxiety to see where the ball is going has probably caused more bad shots than any other single error in golf.

Always bear in mind that power results from co-ordinated, rhythmic body action, not mere brute force. Some of the strongest men and women cannot hit a ball farther than they could shoot a marble, while a little pipsqueak often can whack it two hundred yards or farther with little apparent effort. The purpose of the smooth big swing is to hit the ball accurately and at exactly the split second when the club head has attained its greatest speed and driving power.

The smooth, effortless swing is so important that practically all good golfers hit well "within themselves," as they say. That means that they almost always have reserve power, and try to hit the ball as hard as they can only in rare emergencies. Most of the time they hit about 75 or 80 percent as hard as they can, so they can maintain the smooth, effortless swing that is so essential.

Jack Nicklaus, who is perhaps the strongest great golfer who ever lived, ordinarily drives the ball quite a bit farther than most of the pros he competes against. On the infrequent occasions when he has been forced to cut loose with full power he has been known to shatter the shaft of his driver upon impact. That shows how much power he holds in reserve most of the time.

When you begin play, you will run into days when the game seems almost ridiculously easy. These will be the days when you have put the big swing together into the attractive package it is meant to be—and your putter is working properly. Sometimes these golden days will come when you are physically tired, too tired to make the 100 percent muscular effort that can be so destructive.

Other fine days may come when you are in an "I don't care" frame of mind. This will indicate that you have been under too much tension on bad days and need to relax and play golf as a game, not as a life-and-death matter.

After you have practiced the big swing without a ball until you get the feeling of swinging a weight on a cord every time; after you have perfect confidence that you are assembling all the components properly; after the swing becomes as natural to you as writing your name or walking or any of the other things you have learned to do almost instinctively—without thinking about them—*then* you should take to the driving range to put your acquired skill to good use hitting balls as they should be hit.

Once you are addressing an actual ball with the

intent of sending it flying, *your entire mental attitude must change.* You must concentrate solely and intensely on *hitting the ball.* If you have any doubts about your swing, erase them with a practice swing or two before you actually attempt to hit the ball. Correct all errors then. Do not attempt to make corrections once you have stepped up to actually hit the ball. That is the point of no return and—right or wrong—you must go through the entire process of the big swing with only one thought: hitting the ball.

The old warning, "keep your eye on the ball" should be amplified to "keep your eye *and your mind on the ball.*" Have only one thing in mind: The ball is your target and not an area on the fairway or green. Concentrate on that, and the chances are very good that you will hear the satisfactory "click" that comes when a ball is hit crisply and cleanly.

If you stop to think about the mechanics of the game at any point during the big swing, it will fly to pieces. The time to repair the machinery is before you are trying to hit a ball, not during the process. As well try to change a tire on an Indianapolis Speedway car at 100 miles an hour during a race as to attempt to change your swing during its execution. Thinking about your swing during its progress can result in only one thing: disaster.

On occasion you may see a veritable dub hit the ball solidly after an incongruous swing. The chances are the ball will not go anywhere near where he wants it to because of his bad swing, but it will move, possibly a great distance. When that happens, the dub either has been extremely lucky or he has concentrated intensely on hitting the ball. You can imagine what a beautiful shot he would have had if he had employed the proper swing.

If you don't think concentration is important, just watch the tournament players on television. Quite frequently you will see one of them step away from the ball after he has addressed it because of some minor distraction. This isn't temperament. It is just good business, and golf is a business to these players.

Conversely, you sometimes will see a fine player nonchalantly address the ball—and miss a two-foot putt. Invariably (unless there be some hidden obstacle between his ball and the cup), he misses because his concentration has been broken. He has failed to devote his full attention to the business of hitting the ball.

After you have learned to concentrate on hitting the ball so you can connect solidly, there may still be flaws in your swing that evidence themselves when you "sky" the ball, hook it, slice it, or do any one of the number of things that are the result of an improper swing. As these become apparent, you can correct them (see Chapter Nine, "Correction, Please"), but get rid of the errors by practice. Don't attempt to iron out the wrinkles while you are attempting to hit a ball. You cannot concentrate on both things at the same time; nobody can.

One of the best ways to correct errors in your swing is to see yourself as others see you. This can be done with a home movie camera or—if you are lucky enough to have access to one—even better with a home TV tape outfit. If you are doing anything wrong, it will become instantly apparent when you see yourself in a recorded swing. TV tape has the advantage of instant replay—you can see immediately what you have done wrong. Some of the truly great golfers use film or tape to spot errors that are throwing them off their games. After *winning* the 1972 U. S. Open Championship, Jack Nicklaus carefully studied 5½ hours of tape-recorded replays of himself in the contest to see what he needed to correct in his game.

A very fortunate thing is happening in many cities. Indoor driving ranges are now being equipped with TV tape recording setups. By paying a small fee, you can record your swing as you actually hit a ball and play it back full speed, in slow motion, and in stop motion until you have spotted what you are doing wrong.

It would perhaps be asking too much to ask any student to practice the irons, as well as the woods, before he starts actual play. The urge to get out there and belt one a mile with an easy, effortless big swing is too great.

Even if you don't learn to use the irons and putter before starting actual play, you will step onto the course for your first game with the confidence that goes with knowing full well you can accomplish that most satisfying of all golf shots: the long, straight drive that starts things off with such a bang.

However, driving alone will never make you a good golfer. The woods are full of golfers who can drive the ball out of sight—and straight, too—but fail miserably in the final test, which is recording a low score.

To accomplish that, you must have a well-rounded game.

CHAPTER SIX

The Irons

After you have learned the principles of using the woods, and after the correct big swing has become ingrained so that you can execute it without giving a conscious thought to its mechanics, it is time to turn your attention to the iron clubs.

Although in an ordinary round no one of the irons will be used anywhere nearly as often as the driver or the putter, without mastering their use you cannot play a well-rounded, low-scoring game.

There are three generalities to bear in mind when learning to use the irons:

1. The basic swing that you have become accustomed to—the big swing—serves for all the irons. You merely modify it, principally by changing your stance and shortening your backswing to suit the various clubs of greater loft and shorter range than the woods.

2. You should never *try* to get the ball in the air; *the club does the work.* The loft for each shot is built into the club head, and nothing you can do will make it work better than it will if you bring the club head

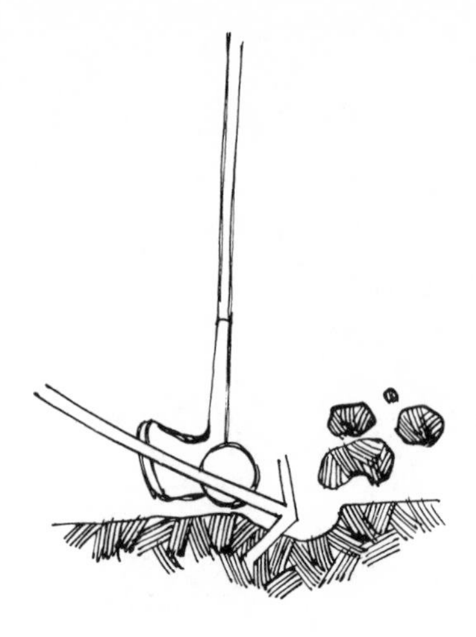

On iron shots blade of club should go through ball on descending blow, taking turf after it has made impact. Divot should be ahead of where ball lay.

into clean, crisp contact with the ball in a rhythmic, coordinated stroke. Anything you may do with your body or hands to try to make the ball fly higher probably will result in complete disaster.

3. On iron shots, the ball should be hit on the downswing rather than after the club head has started to rise. It is mainly to accomplish this that the stance is adjusted for the various iron clubs.

As the distance each iron club is designed to carry decreases, so does the length of the club shaft. As the length of the shaft shortens, it becomes necessary to stand closer to the ball. This can be done properly by standing so that when the arms are fully extended, but not rigid, the entire sole of the club touches the ground. In that position you are addressing the ball at the correct distance.

The Irons

As the range of the club becomes shorter, the ball is played more and more toward the right foot, and the feet come closer and closer together in the stance.

As the loft of the iron used becomes greater—and its range shorter—another adjustment is made: The backswing of the big swing is shortened. Generally speaking, for the long irons (Nos. 1, 2, and 3) the backswing is halted when the club head points to about one or two o'clock. Some carry the backswing for these clubs to the point where the club shaft is horizontal, but virtually no good golfers ordinarily go beyond that point (or over the horizon, as they say) on the backswing for the long irons. The shortened backswing makes for a more compact, accurate stroke and tends to give the player better control of the club.

For shots with the medium irons (Nos. 4, 5, and 6) the backswing is shortened a bit more so that the club head points to twelve o'clock or thereabouts.

For the short irons (Nos. 7, 8, and 9) the backswing can halt at eleven o'clock, or be even shorter, depending on the shot to be made.

These instructions for the length of the backswing are not arbitrary by any means. Except that you should seldom take the long irons beyond the horizontal, they can be altered to suit your taste and comfort and the distance you wish the ball to carry. Whether you tend to underclub or overclub with the irons can be another factor in determining the length of the backswing. If you tend to underclub (employ a club that requires your full effort to carry the distance wanted), then a fuller backswing must be used. If you overclub (use a club that is potentially capable of sending the ball a greater distance than you desire), then the backswing must be shortened.

You probably will find out for yourself, as you practice and play, just how far to bring the club head back to meet varying conditions and achieve definite distances.

If you watch the pros on the tournament circuit, you will notice that they never hit a shot with an iron cleanly off the turf. They always take a divot, and on every effective shot the turf will be dug up just in front of where the ball was lying (this is not true, of course, on teed-up irons shots on the shorter par-three holes).

If you dig up the turf just behind the spot where the ball was lying, it indicates that you have hit the ball on the upswing, after the club head has passed the lowest point in the swing. Perhaps you have done this because you have dipped your head in an effort to scoop up the ball, instead of letting the club do the work for which it was designed. When you do this, you can play havoc with your shot, since a great deal of the momentum is taken out of the club head when it hits the turf before coming in contact with the ball. This not only results in a weakened shot, since the club head is robbed of much of its power before coming into contact with the ball, it can also cause you to lose control of the club and make an indecisive shot.

One of the crucial decisions you must make every time you are faced with an iron shot concerns what club to use, the correct club for the particular condition facing you.

The Irons

The best advice that can be given on this is *don't underclub.* Never select a club that requires an all-out effort to get the ball where you want it. You shouldn't be ashamed to take a No. 6 to reach a distance someone else can achieve with a No. 7 or No. 8 iron. It is much better to overclub a bit—and *play well within yourself* —than to huff and puff and strain and struggle trying to obtain distance with a club having greater loft.

There is no disgrace in using a club designed for greater distance than you need. Quite frequently in professional competition one player will select a longer iron for a distance already achieved by another with a club with less potential distance. If the pros are not ashamed to overclub a bit in order to enjoy a smooth, effortless swing, why should you be? The name of the game is "make the shot," not "play like a big shot." The payoff is on how well you play, not what clubs you play.

The rewards of not being sensitive on this point were made clear by what happened to a fairly good golfer (his scores were consistently in the low nineties and high eighties). This golfer had been playing with a makeshift set of clubs. He finally decided to go to a good pro and be fitted with a well-matched set.

After very careful appraisal, the pro said: "I think you need lighter clubs than you have been using."

"Good," said the golfer. "Give me a set of lighter clubs."

"I hesitate to tell you this," said the pro, "but the best matched set for you happens to be designed for women. They are ladies' clubs."

"I wouldn't care if they were designed for children

or midgets," replied the golfer. "If they'll improve my game, I'll take them."

Fitted with the new clubs, the golfer quickly whittled his score to under ninety consistently—and went right to work trying to break eighty.

Of course, if you don't know the maximum distance you can achieve with each iron, you are likely to underclub badly. The only way you can know exactly what you can get out of each club is to practice with it until you know exactly what you can and cannot make it do under given circumstances.

Start by swinging all out with one particular iron, then reduce the application of power to about 75 or 80 percent. This probably will give you the maximum distance you can achieve with that club under normal conditions, and you should use it for that, or lesser, distances only.

In the following outline of the uses of each iron, the distances given are those within the capabilities of very fine golfers. You can hardly expect to equal them at the outset, if ever. For instance, it is entirely possible, even probable, that for some time to come you will need a No. 2 or No. 3 wood to carry the 210 yards shown for the No. 1 iron or have to use a No. 5 or No. 6 iron to do the work of a No. 8 in more experienced hands.

THE LONG IRONS

The No. 1 iron is for distances up to 210 yards, or even farther when properly used by a very powerful hitter. It is used for lies that make it difficult to hit the ball cleanly with a wood, or when a certain amount of backspin (which is naturally imparted by hitting down on the ball) is desirable to restrict the ball to a short roll after it has landed.

The No. 2 iron is made for distances up to 200 yards and serves much the same purpose as the No. 1. Many pros believe the No. 1 and No. 2 irons are the most difficult of all clubs to use properly and resort to them only when it is imperative to give the ball a fairly high arc of flight or to play it from a difficult lie. Other good players, however, find they can play the ball more accurately with these irons than they can with woods of about equal potentialities.

The No. 3 iron is designed to carry the ball 180 to 190 yards on shots that need a certain amount of backspin, or from a difficult lie, or where a certain amount of loft is required to clear an obstacle.

In taking the stance for the No. 1 iron, the feet should be almost at maximum width, with the ball almost to the left heel. This club may be played from either a square stance or one that is slightly opened or closed, whichever you find most suitable.

The feet are moved slightly closer together in taking the stance for the No. 2 and No. 3 irons, and the ball is played closer to the right foot.

Always bear in mind that the club is designed to do the work of getting the ball into the air. The loft and shaft length of the long irons are in there to give you a long carry with about the same amount of power you would apply for a much shorter distance with a No. 4 or No. 5 iron.

The long irons are played with a nearly full swing and a nearly full turn of the body. In other words, they are played with a slightly curtailed version of the big swing.

THE MEDIUM IRONS

The No. 4 iron is for maximum distances of from 170 to 180 yards, the No. 5 is designed to carry 160 to 170 yards, and the No. 6 is made to send the ball 150 to 160 yards.

Although the No. 4 is, or should be, a very accurate club, its use calls for a fairly full swing and body pivot. It usually is played slightly off center—with the ball toward the left heel—and from a square stance. The feet are placed quite far apart, but not at the maximum. The hands ordinarily are brought back about shoulder high on the backswing when using this club.

The No. 5 iron is used when accuracy begins to be of prime importance. Although it is still a "power" club, it can be used to pinpoint the ball on the target area. It is perhaps the most versatile of all irons, most useful for pitch-and-run shots to the green and for coping with a number of situations. It may be stroked all out for distance or played with a shorter backswing —even a three-quarter swing—for shots requiring greater delicacy.

It is when making "accuracy" shots with the No. 5 iron that the urge to stop the swing short at the moment the club head makes contact with the ball becomes almost irresistible with some players. You should follow through on all strokes, never poke at the ball. Here again it is a case of letting the club do the work for which it was designed, rather than trying to help it by poking it upward. Remember, stick to that basic swing, even in modified form.

It is with the No. 5 iron that the weight begins to stop shifting drastically from left to right, then back again. The weight at address is fairly evenly distributed between the right and left foot, or is slightly on the left foot. The ball is best played squarely between the feet from a square or slightly open stance.

If you are starting with fewer than the permissible maximum of fourteen clubs, the No. 5 iron is the one you probably will find the most useful and handy to have along.

In playing the No. 6 iron, the feet are moved a bit closer together than they are for the No. 5, and the backswing may be shortened a bit to fit your taste and comfort.

THE SHORT IRONS

The No. 7 iron is for distances from 140 to 150 yards, the No. 8 for a maximum of 140 yards, and the No. 9 for anything up to 130 yards.

For the No. 7 the ball is played just a bit off center to the right from a slightly open stance. The No. 8 and No. 9 irons are played pretty much alike from an open stance with the feet only inches apart at the heels, from 6 to 8 inches, or a bit more. The backswing for these irons can vary from almost full to three-quarters of the way or less, depending on what you are trying to achieve.

The No. 9 iron is almost as versatile as the No. 5. It is useful anywhere from a foot off the green (for a pitch and run) to the greater distances of which it is capable. Before the introduction of the wedges, it was the principal weapon from sand traps, very difficult lies, and over obstacles, as well as fairly long approach shots to the green and chip shots.

The ball is played slightly off the right heel with the No. 9. Very little body movement is employed with the No. 8 and No. 9 irons, particularly when they are used for short, delicate precision shots. The swing need not be shortened drastically in making delicate precision shots. Instead, hold the club farther down the grip—"choking" it, as the golfers say.

There is a natural tendency with the shorter-distance clubs to pull the hands in toward the body. This can ruin a shot. The left arm and the club shaft should be in a straight line, as they are for other shots.

It is imperative that the club face be kept square, at right angles to the line of flight for all ordinary iron shots (the club face sometimes is deliberately closed or opened by fine golfers under certain conditions).

It is also important to keep firm control of the club with the grip throughout the swing.

All iron shots (and this seems particularly difficult to do with the shorter irons) should be hit crisply and firmly. A "soft," wishy-washy stroke almost invariably results in a feeble, flabby miss or near-miss.

THE WEDGES

The sand wedge can be used to send the ball anywhere from 100 to 110 yards, and the pitching wedge about 10 yards farther, but both clubs have a multiplicity of uses in the area in between.

Most really good golfers will tell you they use the wedge more than any other club in the bag. They find its adaptability, especially within the scoring zone (under 100 yards from the green) of immense value, not to mention the club's usefulness in getting out of all kinds of trouble. But, of course, they have practiced long and hard to attain the skill that makes this particular club so valuable an asset. And so must anyone to make the wedge pay full dividends.

The wedges have shafts a bit shorter than the No. 9 iron and are quite a bit heavier, perhaps an ounce or more. It is, however, the flange on the sole that gives the wedges their distinction. The wedge extends below the horizontal, giving the wedge the ability to go through the turf or sand without digging in, as the No. 9 iron and other short irons tend to do. This is known to the pros as the club's "bounce."

One of the most helpful uses of the wedge is in making approach shots when not much green is between the cup and the player for the ball to run on. Under such conditions it becomes imperative to stop the ball quickly once it lands. The wedge is designed to impart backspin (provided the ball has been hit on the downswing and turf taken in front of it, as it should be on all iron shots). Much practice is required to determine how much backspin is imparted when

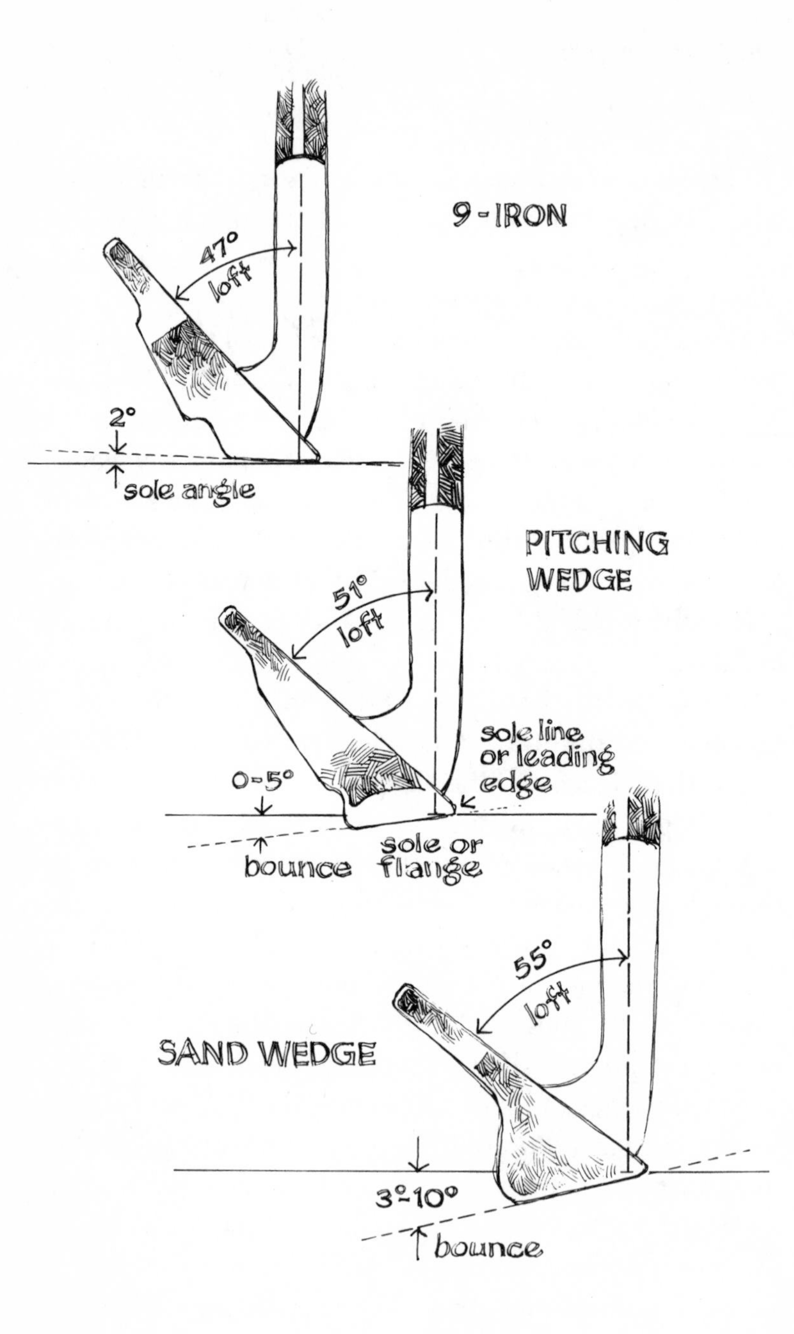
9-IRON
47°
loft
2°
sole angle
PITCHING
WEDGE
51°
loft
sole line
or leading
edge
0-5°
bounce
sole or
flange
55°
loft
SAND WEDGE
3°-10°
bounce

the ball is stroked for various distances and how far the ball will carry.

The No. 9 iron, or one of the other short clubs (depending on the distance from the hole) should be used for approaches where the cup is so placed that there is plenty of running surface on the green between the player and the cup.

Whether to try to make the ball carry almost to the cup, then make an abrupt stop, or to have it hit the putting surface and roll up to the hole is a matter of personal choice. It is worth noting that most of the touring pros seem to prefer sending the ball through the air as near to the cup as possible and checking its course with backspin. You see comparatively few pitch-and-run shots on the tournament circuit. However, whichever type of approach makes you feel the most confident is best for you.

The wedge is very effective for recovery shots from the rough and bad lies. Practice in using the wedge from various types of rough and bad lies will help your game immensely (and usually when you need help) in competition.

Getting out of sand traps is a problem that seems to frighten the average golfer. It shouldn't be. As one pro expressed it, "You don't even have to hit the ball." True, the explosion shot, which sends clouds of sand into the air, is spectacular to look at, but it really is most simple.

To make the explosion shot, take a fairly wide stance (to give you good balance), plant your feet solidly, and hit the sand about an inch behind the ball. Of course, the stroke must be a full one, with plenty of

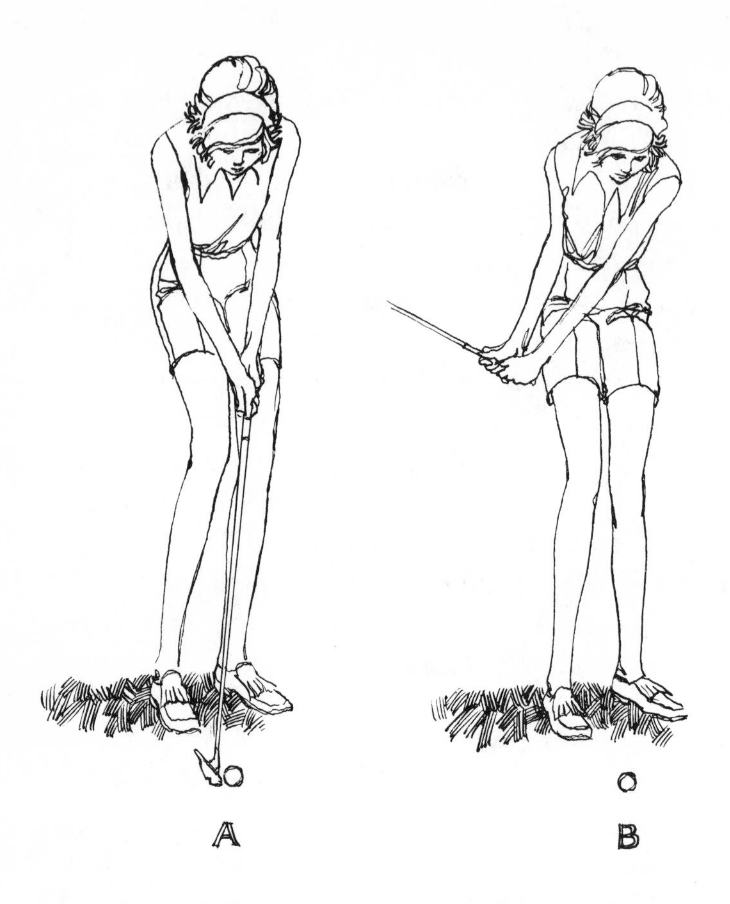

The pitch shot to the green is simplicity itself. At start, weight is on left foot (A). There is little body movement as club is taken back as far as necessary (B).

follow-through. Determining just what club to use and how hard to hit behind the sand in order to lift the ball and send it where you want it is a matter of practice. Just like every other shot in the bag.

It is impossible to overstress the importance of learning to use the irons to full advantage. If there is any one thing that distinguishes a good golfer from a

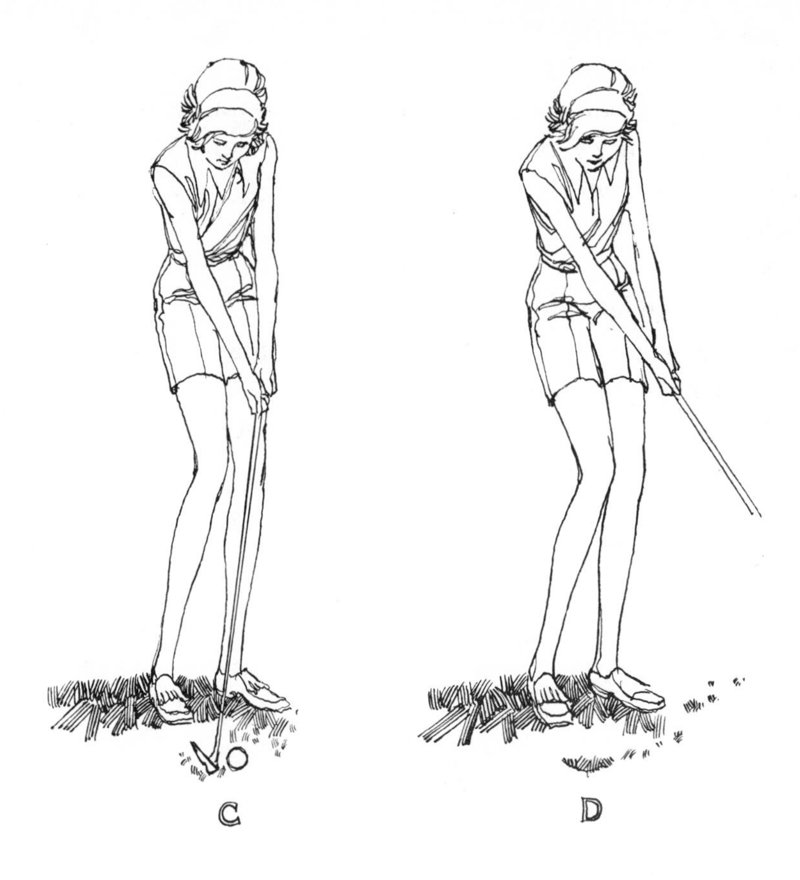

Hit down and through ball (C) and be sure to follow through and not look up until well after ball is hit (D).

truly fine golfer, it is the fine golfer's ability to recover from bad shots (even the finest make bad shots sometimes). The great pros like Nicklaus, Palmer, Littler, and others frequently stun crowds of spectators by their ability to make recovery shots pay off. Faced with seemingly hopeless situations, the big boys blast from sand traps to the cup—and sometimes *into* the cup.

Carried far astray by drives that have gone off course, they play miracle shots over seemingly insurmountable obstacles not only to the green, but often within one-putt distance from the cup.

Such recovery shots are not only essential in preserving a good score, they can prove most disconcerting to an opponent who already has begun to count his golf balls before they were hatched.

The fine golfers never say die, but they have to practice hard to stay alive.

CHAPTER SEVEN

Putting

At first glance, putting looks like the easy part of the game.

Even the figures make it seem simple. The hole is 4.25 inches in diameter, the ball 1.68 inches. Thus the hole is more than 2½ times wider than the ball you are trying to put into it. Actually, the hole is almost an inch (.89 inch) wider than two balls placed together, so it should be fairly easy to hole two regulation golf balls at the same time. The ball doesn't have to be hit squarely to the center of the cup to drop in. It can fall into the hole if more than half of it is over the cup. This adds another .75 inch of "drop in" area on each side of the cup, so your target is almost four times as wide as the ball you are trying to put into it.

So what's so difficult about getting a little thing like a golf ball into a hole with all that room to spare?

The answer? All sorts of things. Such as nerves, temperament, the weather, contoured greens, the texture of the grass, and things like that. But mainly, the sheer perversity of this part of the game. That's what is so frustrating—and fascinating—about putting.

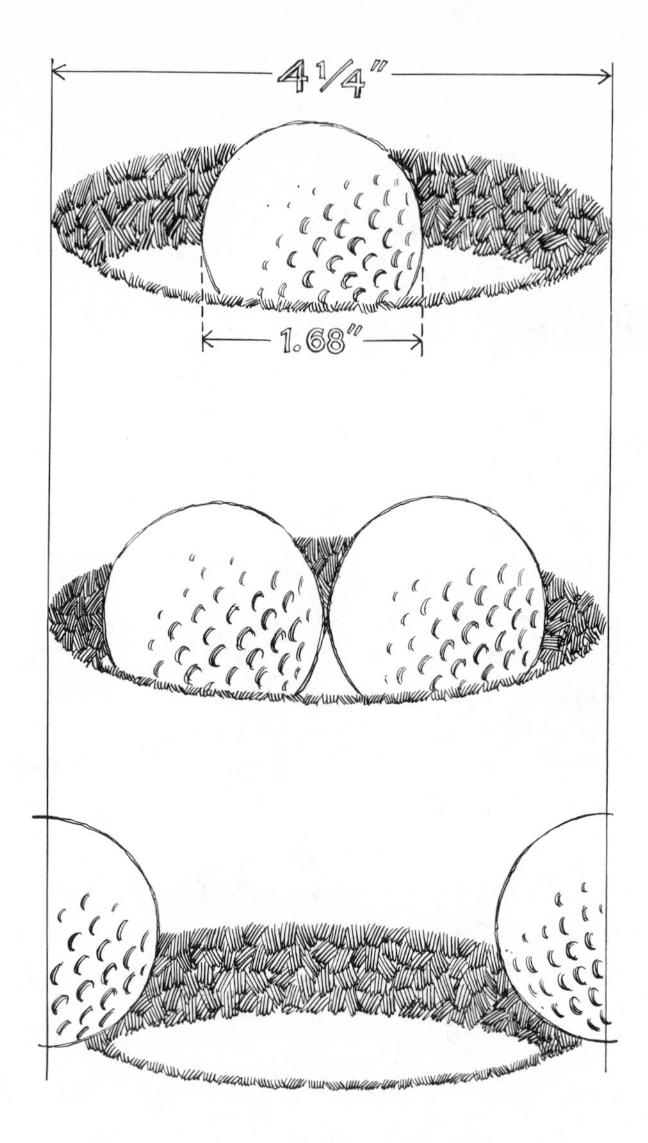

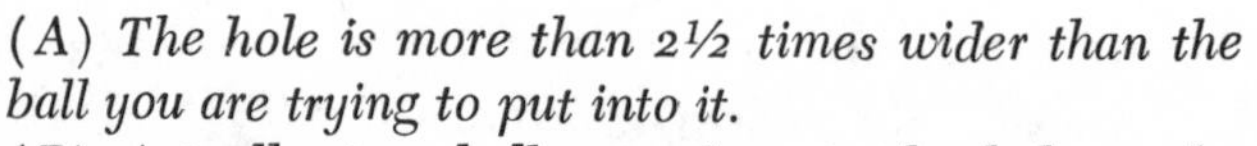

(A) The hole is more than 2½ times wider than the ball you are trying to put into it.
(B) Actually, two balls can drop in the hole at the same time, with almost an inch to spare.
(C) If half the ball is over the hole, it can drop in. This adds another three-quarters of an inch of target area on each side of the cup.

Putting

Nobody has yet devised the absolutely right way to putt, nor can anyone define the wrong way. There are as many working styles of putting as there are putters, and they range from the sublime to the ridiculous. On the greens even the ridiculous works for some people—sometimes.

Leo Diegel, a star of the 1920s, used to bend way over the ball with his arms askew as though he were about to milk a cow. To everyone's amazement—sometimes even his own—Diegel did very well in this absurd posture, swinging his arms back and forth like a pendulum to hole difficult putts with a dangling putter with remarkable regularity.

Sam Snead, who occupies a niche in the PGA Hall of Fame, won the PGA and the Masters three times and the British Open once, but he could never come out ahead in the U. S. Open. He finished second four times in that big one, largely because his putting—never one of Slammin' Sammy's strongest points—was not up to par.

Sam always was proud that in his day he was the oldest man ever to win a PGA tour event. In 1961, when he was just days away from being forty-nine, he won the Tournament of Champions.

Snead returned to the professional circuit in 1971–72 and did quite well indeed for a man nearing sixty. He returned to the wars because he had discovered a new, to him, way of putting, using a club that looked as though it had been in a bad automobile crash and using a freakish, croquet style of stroking the ball.

So what kind of putting style should you adopt? The one that suits you best. You just "grab your best holt" and start to wrestle with the problem.

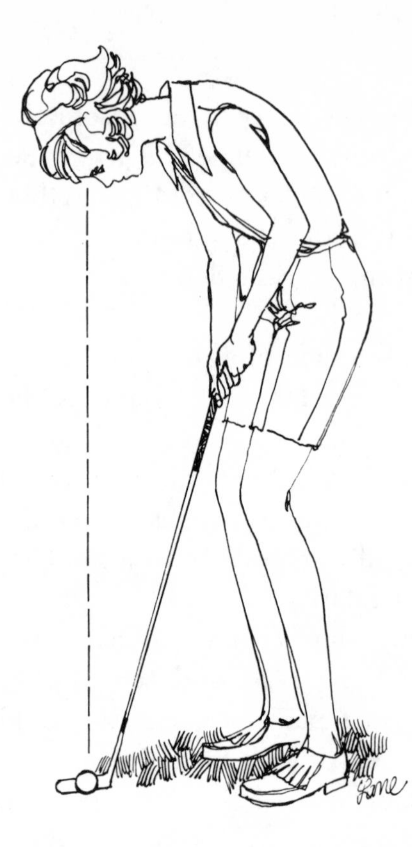

Good putters keep their eyes directly over back of ball, have blade of putter square to line of flight, sole flat to ground.

There are several basic principles that seem to help all putting, no matter how weird the style.

There are many different grips used in putting, some very extreme, others in which the player makes only minor, if any, adjustments in his regular manner of holding the club. It is suggested that you start out with your regular grip—the one you have grown accustomed to in the big swing, the one that should have become second nature to you by now. As you go along, you may wish to make modifications, a minor change here and there or even a revolutionary revision. Many teaching pros recommend that the regular grip be retained in putting, so that it will not feel foreign when you return to it for clubs other than the putter. However, that's entirely up to you. Do whatever makes you feel the most comfortable and gives you the greatest confidence on the green.

All good putters keep their eyes directly over the back of the ball, on the spot where they aim to hit the ball. Usually their necks are parallel to the ground. To achieve this, some bend at the waist until their upper bodies are practically parallel to the ground. Others stand more erect. Again, this is a matter of personal choice and whatever makes you feel more confident and comfortable.

The blade of the putter should be square to the intended line to the target at impact. Some good golfers open the blade on the backswing, but almost without exception they hit the ball squarely. The simplest way to do this is to keep the blade square to the line throughout the swing. This can be done easily by keeping the back of the left hand toward the target throughout and by keeping the left hand behind the right (don't roll the wrists) until after the ball has been hit.

The sole of your putter should lie flat on the ground when you take your stance, and good putters usually keep the blade low to the ground throughout the putting stroke.

The body should be in a solid, comfortable position

All putts should be carefully surveyed before ball is addressed.

for putting. Some achieve this by keeping their weight well back on their heels. Others employ more stringent methods. Arnold Palmer, for instance, stands knock-kneed and pigeon-toed, his knees close together to give him a feeling of solidity and firmness.

Most good putters keep the action close to the body, their hands in close throughout the putt.

Some golfers use their arms in the putting swing, others only the hands and wrists, but most seem to agree that the body should not move at any time during the stroke. All the power needed for even the longest of putts can be supplied by either the arms or the hands or both. Body power is not needed.

Two things all good putters unanimously agree on. It is just as important to keep your head down and your eye and mind on the ball in putting as it is in any other stroke. It is also of crucial importance that you do not change your mind or have any doubts about what you intend to do once you have started your putt. Decide how you are going to play the putt before you address the ball, then don't change your mind. To become confused and try to change course during the putting stroke can result in utter chaos.

All putts should be carefully surveyed before the ball is addressed. Look at the area between the ball and the cup from the side to determine roughly whether the contour of the green requires a slow, medium, or fast trip for the ball. Then determine the line of flight from behind the ball.

At this point it is a good idea to examine closely and repair (within the limits allowed by the rules) the line of the putt.

On the putting green a ball may be lifted and cleaned without penalty and the player may remove any loose impediments by lifting or brushing them aside with his hand or club, provided he does not press anything down. The damage caused to the green by the impact of a ball may also be repaired, but spike marks in the line of flight may not be pressed down or otherwise repaired. With those exceptions, the line of putt must not be touched, but the player may place his club in front of the ball in addressing it, providing he does not press anything down.

Many well-hit and well-directed putts, which seem to be headed straight for the hole, go awry at the end of their run toward the cup. They waver or go astray in the last few feet. This can be caused by the rim of the cup, or lip of the hole, rising because of contraction of the soil around the cup. Since nothing can be pressed down on the green, there is nothing to do under these circumstances except to hit the ball a bit harder to give it momentum to get over the incline.

The pros examine the grass for two or three feet around the cup before putting. If it looks heavy—the kind to slow up the ball as it nears the end of its run—they aim for the back of the cup and take a little harder swipe at the ball than they would ordinarily. If the grass is slick or sparse—the kind that offers little resistance to the ball—they allow for the ball's acceleration as it nears the cup.

Although there is nothing like experience for learning how to "read" a green, there are a few standard methods of determining whether the surface is fast, medium, or slow. The speed of the green can roughly be determined by weather conditions and how long the grass has been allowed to grow. A more esoteric reading can be gained from knowledge of the characteristics of the various types of grasses ordinarily used on greens and also by determining how the grain of the grass grows.

Of course, uncut grass slows the ball and requires a firmer tap than a new-mown surface, which tends to speed up the ball in transit. In the morning, when the grass is moist, greens tend to be slower than they are later in the day when the grass has dried out. An uncut green played early in the morning can be very slow and require a much harder tap of the ball than it will be after the sun has dried things off and the lawn mower has been at work.

Greens in predominantly dry areas tend to be much faster than those where there is a great deal of rain and moisture. Drainage also affects the speed of the greens.

A ball rolls faster and with less motive power when it goes with the grain, i.e., in the direction that the flat-lying blades point. The grain usually grows away from higher ground, just as water would flow off the same surface, or grain may follow the prevailing winds if they are steady and strong enough. On oceanside courses the grain usually runs toward the ocean.

Putts across the grain tend to break in the direction the grass lies.

The more generally used types of grass on greens are bent, rye, and Bermuda.

Greens of bent grass tend to be fast, since the narrow blades can be cut very short. Bent has comparatively little grain. This type of grass grows very well where the climate is fairly moist year around. It is widely used in the United States along both seacoasts and in the north.

Rye grass, which probably makes the best putting surface, is a temperate zone grass. It will not grow well during hot, humid southern summers or during moist winters in the north.

Bermuda grass grows where once there were only sand greens, so well does it thrive in hot climates. It is used extensively in the South, Southwest, the Caribbean, and in Southern California. Because it is heavy-grained, most golfers find it an exceedingly difficult and tricky putting surface until they become accustomed to reading it properly and making the necessary adjustments.

When determining how hard to stroke a putt over a contoured green, bear in mind that as the speed of the ball decreases it becomes more responsive to the downward pull on an undulation. Thus if the cup lies at the top of a rise, the ball must be stroked to compensate for the downward drag. Conversely, if the cup lies at the bottom or on the downward side of an undulation, the ball must be stroked lighter. Sheer momentum sometimes will carry the ball from the top of a rise to the cup when it lies at the bottom.

One of the most common mistakes made on the green is to not pay full attention to each and every putt. You will see many golfers who spend hours and hours practicing their big swings, irons, recoveries, and other phases of the game, only to step up and hurriedly—almost nonchalantly—miss a putt because their attention wasn't riveted on the business at hand.

Putting

Contrast the hit-or-miss attitude of the average golfer with the careful study and preparation Jack Nicklaus makes before even addressing a comparatively easy putt. Nicklaus never merely steps up to a putt and strokes it. Before he hits the ball he has considered every aspect of the green and knows exactly what he hopes to achieve once he strokes the ball.

Granted that Nicklaus is a slow player, slow as only the very great have a right to be. If an ordinary player took as much time preparing for every shot as Nicklaus does, the players behind him—or even those playing with him—would set up a clamor, and rightfully. However, there is no reason why you or any other player should be rushed into making a putt without making at least cursory preparations.

As someone has said, it is an unalterable fact of life that a two-foot putt counts just as much as a 250-yard drive. Putts make up half, at least, of all strokes played in a round. They should *all* be treated with great respect and never sloughed off.

Proper practice is essential to the cultivation of good putting, as it is to the rest of the game. Practice putts should be varied. Don't just stand in one spot and keep shooting for the cup. Vary the distances you attempt and the conditions under which the putt must be holed. If you find you have developed a definite pattern of missing—such as going too far to the left or right, being short or overshooting—work on the problem until you discover what you are doing wrong to cause the ball to go off course.

Indoor practice on a carpet can be helpful, but it also can impart false confidence because the carpet has no grain and the floor is not contoured.

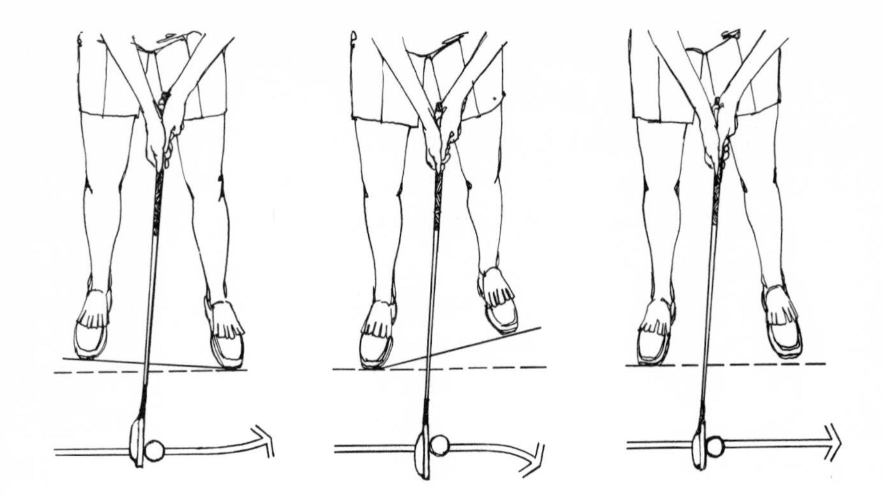

Figure 1, Figure 2, Figure 3.

Whether a golfer should concentrate on distance rather than direction when putting is a moot point. Most good putters will tell you they pay more attention to sending the ball the proper distance than they do on direction. It is probably nearer the truth to say that they concentrate equally on both important aspects of the putt. The really good pros on the tournament tour seem determined to sink *every* putt, no matter from how great a distance. That is probably the main reason they come up with so many seemingly miraculous shots on the green.

Some fine putters say they visualize the path of the ball, sometimes actually picture it going into the cup before they have even stroked it. Try this yourself. It may help, if only through the power of suggestion.

Other good putters will tell you that on long putts they don't aim for the cup itself, but for a spot between the ball and the cup, and try to reach that spot at a speed that will carry the ball to its intended destination.

Whether to use the putter or an iron for a pitch-and-run shot from the fringe or the grass growing around the green is a matter for determination in each individual situation. It is worth noting that the tournament players seem to prefer using the putter—or Texas wedge, as they call it—whenever they can under these conditions.

A few tips from the tournament pros may prove useful in achieving good putting:

1. Grass always seems more shiny and lighter when you look at it with the grain, darker when you look against the grain.

2. Downhill putts "break" more with contour and grain than uphill putts.

3. Have the club head accelerating at impact to secure a firm, crisp contact with the ball.

4. The best place to practice is on a regular green on a standard course, if you can find a layout where this is permitted at a time when it will not interfere with regular play.

5. Putting on an absolutely flat green or eighteen-hole putting courses is not as beneficial as practice on a regular green. Some courses have additional contoured greens set aside for practice.

6. Adjusting your stance can help to compensate for contour or other breaks that make a straight-line putt ineffective. Normally, with feet in a square stance, both toes parallel to the line of roll (Figure 1), a

straight putt results. The ball may be sent toward the left by closing the stance (Figure 2) and playing the ball slightly toward the toe of the club, with the hands a bit ahead of the ball. Bringing the left foot back in an open stance and playing the ball toward the heel of the putter (Figure 3) will send the ball toward the right to counteract a break to the left.

7. For those who simply cannot judge how hard to stroke a putt to send it the proper distance, the "inch for foot" method sometimes proves helpful. In this system, the club head is brought back an inch on the backswing for every foot you wish to propel the ball. Thus, for a ten-foot putt, you would bring the club back ten inches on the backswing. This method works only on greens in average condition, if it works at all.

CHAPTER EIGHT

Mind over Matter

Golf is a thinking man's game. Not so much as chess or bridge or other strictly cerebral pastimes, but certainly more than most athletic competition.

In golf, every competitor has three opponents: himself, the course, and the golfer or golfers he is matched against.

No sport requires more self-control than golf. To achieve the utmost satisfaction and best scores in the game, you must discipline yourself to hours and hours of practice.

You must think out your problems *before* you address the ball—then erase all such thoughts and *concentrate completely* on hitting the ball. After a shot is made—whether it be good or bad—forget it and begin to think of the future. Accept the bad shot gracefully and rearrange your plans to make up for it. Be confident but not overconfident. Control your temper. Blowups from bad temper probably have ruined as many golf games as misplayed shots.

If all this sounds as though you must be a paragon of self-control to play good golf, that's exactly what it means. You cannot play the best golf of which you are physically capable if you lose, and not use, your head.

Practically all professional golfers have trained themselves, if they weren't already so inclined, to think positively. They always concentrate on what they wish to accomplish, not what they must avoid. For instance, on the tee with a huge bunker within shooting distance on the right, the pro doesn't say to himself, "I must avoid that bunker at all costs." Instead, he picks a safe spot away from the danger zone and concentrates on sending the ball to that area. It is a strange quirk of golfing psychology that the more one thinks about the risk of landing a ball in a certain spot, the more likely it becomes that the ball will take off in that direction.

The course is an opponent because it has been planned that way. It is the aspiration of every golf architect to lay out a course that is as difficult as possible to play, but eminently fair. No good golf architect will deliberately lay out a course with hazards and rough in areas where they will trap a good shot, but he will contrive to put the most fiendish obstacles he can think of in areas where they will penalize a bad shot.

The good golfer always has a clear mental picture of how he wishes to play a hole *before* he addresses the ball. If a course is new to him, he will survey it from the tee and ask questions about the lay of the land before he makes his plans. If they can, the touring professionals always walk a course before playing it in competition. They even pace off distances between points, test sand in traps, and examine the fairway, rough, and greens grass minutely.

Mind over Matter

After you have surveyed the hole from the tee, plan each shot. If, somewhere along the line, the ball fails to land where you intended it to be, revise your plans accordingly and continue to play as though nothing had gone awry.

Tournament golfers, who always try to hit away from trouble, have discovered an interesting fact. They find that if they tee up on the side nearest the trouble, it helps them shoot away from it. In other words, if the trouble lies on the right of the fairway, they tee up as far to the right as is permissible for their drive. For some reason, perhaps psychological, they find that if they tee up on the left of the tee they tend to drive toward the right—or in the direction of the trouble they are seeking to avoid.

In approach shots a good golfer will, if he possibly can, aim for the cup, but he always tries to figure his shot so that if he fails to hole out or come near the cup, he will be in an advantageous position for his next shot. For instance, aiming for a cup that is on a contour of the green, the good player will always plan his approach shot to wind up where he has an uphill, rather than a downhill, lie for his next shot.

One of the decisions that must be made time after time is whether to play boldly or with caution on a specific shot. Say your drive lands in difficult rough in a fairly bad lie. You have two choices. You can play a wood or long iron boldly toward the hole for distance —and run the risk of winding up still in the rough and in a bad lie. Or you can sacrifice distance for safety and use a wedge or other short iron to get in the fairway with a good lie.

Here, several factors must be taken into consideration. Some players are just naturally bold, others cautious—and probably will follow their natural inclinations no matter what the circumstances. Careful consideration, however, might dictate a course of action contrary to their natural inclinations.

If you have a comfortable lead over your opponent, then probably you should play it safe, be content just to get out of trouble. However, if you cannot afford to sacrifice a stroke, then you must play the bold shot. Say a match play game is dormie—your opponent two holes up with two to play—then the bold play is your only hope, barring a sudden blowup on the part of your opponent.

Applying *gentlemanly* psychological pressure against an opponent is part of the game, but unsportsmanlike "goat-getting" is not. Walter Hagen, as great a competitive golfer as ever lived, might find it difficult to get away today with some of the stunts he pulled to befuddle an opponent.

In one important round at match play, the Haig conceded every putt under two feet until a crucial ten-incher came up toward the end of the game. When the opponent automatically stooped to pick up the ball, Hagen insisted he play it out. The flustered opponent missed the short putt—and Hagen won the important match. The ploy was strictly legal, but certainly unsportsmanlike.

Perhaps the best way to apply psychological pressure is to play better than your opponent. Certainly if you can remain calm and unflustered when things go wrong, it has a disconcerting effect on your opponent.

Mind over Matter

A good recovery shot that takes you out of a difficult situation can be very unnerving to an opponent who had already counted you out. It also tends to upset an opponent—and is very good conduct—not to seem unhappy when an opponent makes a particularly good shot.

The tournament pros play for an honest psychological advantage whenever they can, especially on the green, where pressure tends to mount to the breaking point. Quite frequently a golfer on the green, away by many feet from the cup, will putt to within striking distance of the hole, well within his opponent's ball. It is now the player's choice either to continue to putt until he holes out, or to lift his ball and mark the spot while the opponent shoots for the cup. That is where psychology comes in. If the player is a good putter and feels in fine form, he probably will elect to hole out. If he sinks the putt, the opponent must drop a much longer putt or lose a stroke. Thus the player has put the pressure on his opponent.

If the player is not confident of his ability to hole out, he can lift and mark—giving his opponent no alternative but to hole out lest he run the risk of dropping a stroke.

Of course, either ploy can backfire. The player may fail to sink his putt if he elects not to lift and mark, thus throwing the pressure back on himself. Or the opponent may plop the longer putt into the cup, thus putting greater pressure on the player when it comes his time to shoot again.

The three forces that gang up on a player—himself, the course, and the opposing player—make quite a formidable enemy. They seem determined to get the player. The only thing the player can do is be equally determined to exert great self-control, and plan his campaign against the course and, of course, his opponent.

Some very fine golfers will tell you that they always play the course and par, even in a head-to-head match. It is doubtful if even the most disciplined players can manage this completely, but you can try. And the closer you come to doing it, the better are your chances of winning.

CHAPTER NINE

Correction, Please

No matter how well the golfer plans each shot, there will be times when he gets in trouble. To be a good golfer, you must learn to accept the difficult situation philosophically and not let it throw you off your stride. "Blowing up" over one bad break can explode your entire game. So let us try to learn how to cope with the most common difficult situations—the ones that usually come from your having made some basic mistake.

One of the most common difficult situations that can arise is finding your ball on an uphill or downhill lie. Uphill and downhill lies are almost inevitable on all but the flattest of courses. Sometimes they can be avoided. It is often advantageous to the golfer to hit a somewhat shorter shot than he is capable of just to avoid landing his ball in an uphill or downhill lie.

However, no matter how you try to avoid them, sooner or later you will land on an uphill or downhill lie. When you do, there is one rule to remember: Always take your stance with the ball nearer the foot that is higher than it would be from a flat lie. In other words, from an uphill lie, play the ball more toward your left foot, because your center of gravity is forward and there should be more weight on the left foot. From a downhill lie, play the ball off the right foot. This practice of relating the ball to your feet assures you of missing the ground before hitting the ball on an uphill lie and lets you hit the ball before hitting the ground on a downhill lie.

There is a tendency to hook from an uphill lie, so aim your shot a bit toward the right. A downhill lie tends to produce a slice, so aim your shot a little to the left.

An uphill lie changes the loft of your shot, sending the ball higher and not as far as it would go from a flat lie. To compensate for this, take a club with more loft than you would ordinarily (e.g., a distance that would require a No. 7 iron ordinarily will need to be played with a No. 6 or No. 5 from an uphill lie). A downhill lie tends to diminish the loft of the club, so take one club less from such a position.

Topping the ball is one of the most common mishaps that can happen to the dub golfer, and sometimes even good players are guilty of the error. A topped ball makes a sudden dive, then hops along the ground for a very short distance. If you top the ball consistently, go over your big swing, bit by bit. The chances are that you will find that instead of keeping your head in the same position relative to the ball throughout, you are swaying your body and moving your head from side to side or bobbing it up and down. You have lost your "weight on a cord" swing and must regain it.

Sometimes topping is caused by bending over too

much at address (instead of taking the slight "sit-down" position). This, too, causes the club head to get out of the smooth arc of the big swing, because the golfer who bends over too much at address tends to straighten up on the backswing and bring the club back on a different arc on the downswing.

Hitting under the ball causes it to go too high. This is called "skying." This fault, too, results from a flaw in the basic big swing, which you must discover on the practice tee. It is also possible that you have developed the habit of skying because you have forgotten the basic rule of keeping your eyes—and your mind—on the ball.

Slicing is perhaps the most common fault of the high-scoring golfer. On the average course, especially on a weekend, you will see more slices than you can find in a delicatessen.

There are slices and slices, some good, most of them bad. A ball that starts out straight, then veers to the right toward the end of its flight is said to "fade." Many good golfers fade their tee shots consistently, with no bad effects because they allow for the deviation from the straight and narrow when aiming their shots.

A full-grown slice is a different matter. The ball starts curving to the right from the start, more like a boomerang than a golf ball. This true slice can be most dangerous, carrying the ball into rough, hazards, out of bounds, and almost anywhere but where the golfer intends it to go. Even if it doesn't wind up in trouble, a sliced ball robs the player of distance.

A slice is caused by doing one of two things wrong. The most common error is hitting from the outside-in, slicing the club head across the ball at impact. This imparts a spin clockwise—much like the "English" applied intentionally to a billiard ball—which misdirects the flight of the ball.

Hitting across the ball can usually be corrected by drawing the right foot back an inch or so at address. It may be that your slice comes from not returning your right elbow to the right side quickly enough on the downswing.

You may also be slicing because your grip has become sloppy. Check to see that the V formed by your thumbs and index fingers are pointing toward your right shoulder. When this V points to the left, it can cause the outside-in action that results in the club cutting across the ball and imparting the clockwise spin that makes slices.

Slicing can also be caused by hitting the ball with an open club face instead of squarely. This may cause a slice even though the ball is hit in a straight line. If you suspect that this is the trouble, check your big swing carefully and you probably will find that you are getting your body and hands too far ahead of the club head at the precise moment you hit the ball or that you are failing to shift your weight to your right foot at the beginning of your backswing.

Hooking is a less common fault with the average golfer than slicing. A slight hook, called a "draw," takes the ball to the left from its straight path toward the end of its flight. The draw can be compensated for and is employed regularly by many good golfers. A complete hook is the opposite of the full slice. It sends the ball sharply toward the left from the moment of

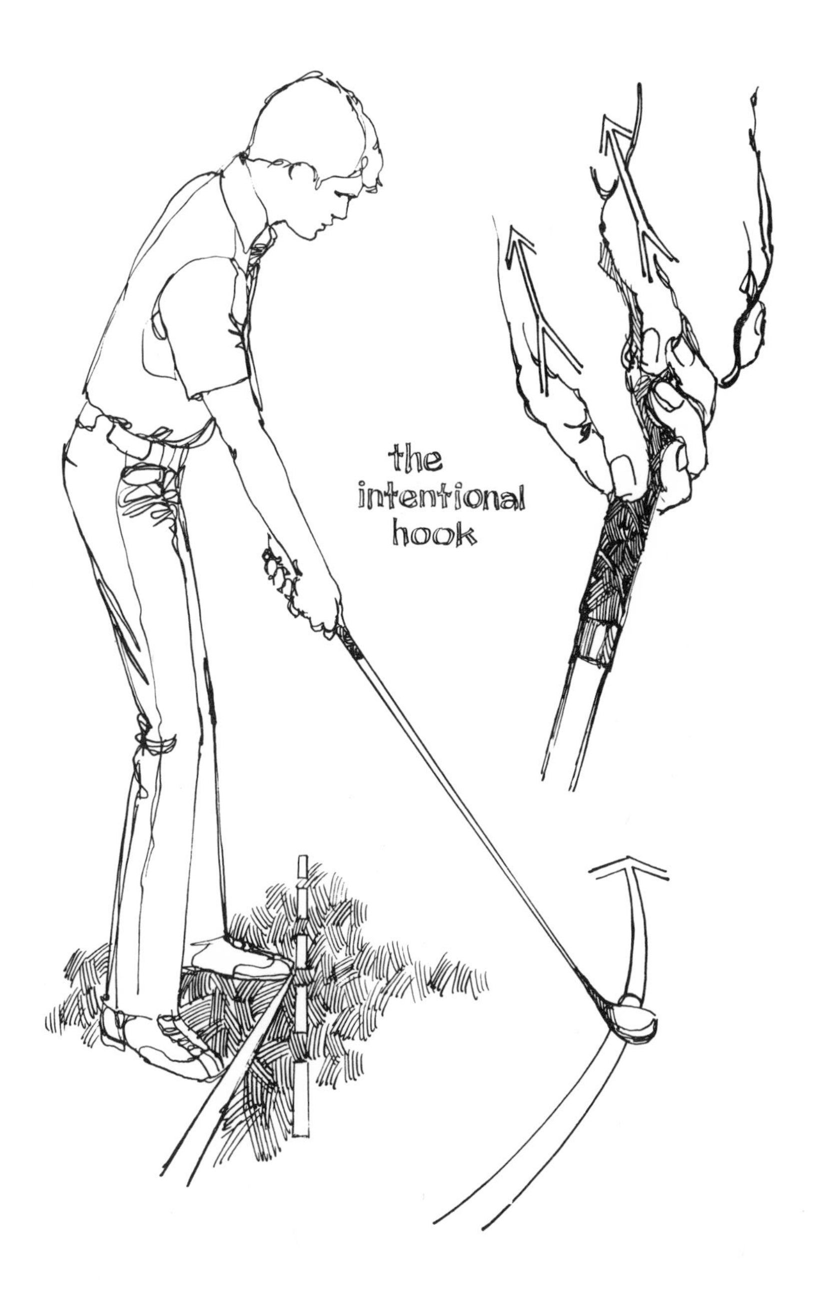
the
intentional
hook

the
intentional
slice

impact. This fault usually begins early in the downswing when the golfer fails to shift his weight to the left foot at the start or starts swinging too soon in the downswing. Both these errors can cause the hands to roll over, bringing the club head into contact with the ball in a closed, or toed-in position.

Hooking also can result from a faulty grip, with the V formed by the thumbs and forefingers pointing too far to the right, instead of directly at the right shoulder.

Golfers who are far enough advanced to play intentional slices and hooks to get around trouble usually achieve these shots by adjusting their grips. For a hook, they arrange the hands so they can see the knuckles of all four fingers on the left hand. For a slice, they grip the club so they can see only the knuckle on the first finger of the left hand.

For a deliberate slice, the golfer intentionally swings from the outside-in, and from the inside-out for a hook.

Generally speaking, when any consistent flaw develops in your game, you should go back to the practice range and take your big swing apart and look it over carefully piece by piece to discover what you are doing wrong. Somewhere along the line you are deviating from the smooth, rhythmic "weight on a cord" big swing.

CHAPTER TEN

Etiquette

A philosophical sportsman has said there are only three ways to get to really know a person; spend two weeks with him on a hunting trip, a weekend on a small boat, or eighteen holes on the golf course.

The very nature of the game seems to bring out the best—and the worst—in Everyman. Irascible tycoons who growl at old ladies, snap at office boys, and throw things at faithful secretaries can become mild-mannered and affable on the golf course, especially if their game is going well. Know-it-alls in the business world become silly putty in the hands of their pros. Hard-hearted financiers, who will foreclose a mortgage at the drop of a payment, overtip caddies and clubhouse attendants.

On the other hand, timorous little underlings can become raging lions in an argument over a golf score or rule interpretation, and meek little men who wouldn't swat a mosquito elsewhere have been known to throw golf clubs at small birds who have dared to emit one peep while they were attempting a crucial putt.

Etiquette

Perhaps because of the intense concentration called for in golf, thoughtless, boorish, or other untoward conduct is more distracting and upsetting on the course than anywhere else. A mere word or unnecessary movement at the wrong time can throw another player's drive or putt out of whack. Just standing in the wrong place sometimes can shatter another's concentration.

Jack Nicklaus is cool, calm, phlegmatic, and completely untemperamental—an almost unflappable competitor. Yet he has been known to walk away from a shot he was preparing to make (good-naturedly, of course) until some minor commotion or other distraction has been repressed.

In general, the Golden Rule applies in golf etiquette as it does in all common courtesy. Do unto others, etc., never worked better than it does on the course.

Golf is not a somber game, by any means, yet it is taken seriously by many. Loud talk, warwhoops of exultation, displays of temper, and other distracting exhibitions are out of place. In golf, if there is anything worse than a sore loser it is a sore winner; don't sulk or gloat over the way your game happens to be going.

Some more or less formal etiquette is actually part of the rules, although there is no penalty for violations other than the loss of respect of your fellow players.

The more generally observed no-nos are:

1. Don't talk, move, or stand close to or directly behind another player's ball while he is addressing it or making a stroke.

2. Let the player who has the honor or is entitled to play before you, finish his shot before you tee up or

assume your stance at your ball. Stand behind the line of play or well out of it.

3. Don't play until the players ahead of you are well out of range, have at least made their second shots from the fairway. Don't shoot to the green until the match in advance have left the area. Shooting into a match is not only extremely discourteous, it can be dangerous. Even the veriest novice can sometimes hit the ball a surprising distance, so if in doubt—wait!

4. Replace and press down all turf or sod displaced by your club in making a shot (such turf or sod is called a divot). Fill up all holes made by you in a bunker. Repair all damage made by you to the putting green before leaving the green.

5. Don't rush—golf is not a rushing game—but play all shots promptly and leave the green immediately after all players in your match have holed out. Post-mortems shouldn't be held on the green if there is a match following. However, it isn't nice to leave the green, or its apron, until everyone in your match has putted out.

6. Don't drop, or allow your caddy to drop, your bag on the putting green or where it might interfere with another's play.

7. If your match is looking for a lost ball, signal other matches behind you to pass (play through). Once you have signaled a following match to play through, don't resume play until players in that match are well out of range. (There is a specific rule for time allowed to search for a lost ball.)

8. Don't stand so your shadow is cast on another's ball while he is making a stroke, especially on the green.

9. Try never to walk in the line of another player's putt and, in general, "tread lightly" on the green to avoid marring the turf with the spikes of your shoes.

10. If your match is slow and falls more than one hole behind (allows more than one clear hole to come between it and the match ahead), the match following has the right to, and should be, signaled to play through.

Scorecards usually carry local ground rules for the course being played, and some have a summary of the more important universal rules, but it is well to carry a copy of the USGA rules in case exceptional conditions arise.

Remember, golf rules are not promulgated to hamper play, but rather to add to the enjoyment of the pastime and circumvent argument.

CHAPTER ELEVEN

Rules

Golf is one game in which rules were not made to be broken. As Joseph C. Dey, Jr., who was custodian of rules for the United States Golf Association (he now is a big wheel with the Professional Golfers Association) has so often pointed out, golf rules have been made to help, not hamper, the player.

Over the years that the game has been developing from a simple Scottish peasant pastime golf has evolved rules for almost every contingency, but such is the variety of surprises the recreation affords that from time to time situations arise that require expert consideration. That is why quite frequently you will see someone like Dey called into consultation to settle some unique and puzzling problem of procedure.

Of course, nobody expects a player to be a "sea lawyer" (one who has all the rules at his fingertips and is constantly invoking them), but it is a good thing to know the fundamental rules of correct procedure for situations that arise with more or less frequency.

The scorecards for most courses show local rules and the general USGA rules, but it is well to have a knowledge beyond that if you are playing regularly.

Rules

The ones that follow should get you by under most circumstances.

It is well to remember that the official rules never refer to the fairway or rough, but use the general term "through the green" to cover both.

Except when otherwise specified or specifically stated that there is another penalty, the penalty for a breach of a USGA or local rule is loss of hole in match play and loss of two strokes in stroke (or medal) play.

During the play of a hole it is against the rules to play a practice stroke. Between the play of two holes, it is permitted to play practice strokes, but not from a hazard or to any green but the one last played. Penalty: Match play, loss of hole. Stroke play, two strokes. In stroke play the penalty is applied to the next hole.

Note: A practice *swing* (in which a ball is not hit) is not a practice *stroke*. A practice swing may be taken any place on the course, provided it does not violate some other rules.

Except on the putting green (see rule for putting) a player may have the line of play indicated to him by anyone, but no mark may be placed on the line, nor may anyone stand on or close to the line while the stroke is being played. Penalty: Match play, loss of hole. Stroke play, two strokes.

In match play, a player who plays from the tee ahead of turn may be required by his opponent to abandon that ball and play another, without penalty. There is no penalty in stroke play for playing out of turn.

Any loose impediment may be removed without penalty except when both the impediment and the ball lie in or touch a hazard. The penalty for moving an impediment in a hazard is loss of hole in match play, two strokes in stroke play.

However, through the green if the ball moves after any loose impediment lying within a club length of it has been touched by the player, his partner, or either of their caddies, the player touching the impediment will be penalized one stroke and the ball must be played as it lies.

The penalty for playing the wrong ball, except in a hazard, is loss of the hole in match play, two strokes in stroke play. There is no penalty for playing the wrong ball from a hazard, provided the right ball is then played and the other ball replaced where it was.

In dropping a ball under the rules, a player must face the hole, stand erect, and drop the ball behind him over his shoulder. If the ball is dropped in any other manner, then played, a penalty stroke is incurred.

If a ball dropped in this manner rolls out of bounds, into a hazard, or more than two club lengths from the point where it first struck the ground, it will be redropped without penalty.

If a dropped ball comes to rest nearer to the hole than its original position, it must be redropped without penalty. If the configuration of the ground makes it impossible to prevent a dropped ball from coming to rest nearer the hole, it will be placed, without penalty.

Except in a hazard a player may lift his ball for identification, in the presence of his opponent. It must be placed on the spot from which it was lifted.

A ball may be cleaned when lifted from an unplayable lie, for relief from an obstruction, from casual water, ground under repair, from a water hazard, or on the putting green.

Otherwise, during the playing of a hole a player may not clean a ball except to the extent necessary for identification or if permitted by local rule. Penalty: match play, loss of hole; stroke play, two strokes.

Through the green or in a hazard, a player may have any other ball lifted if he considers that it might interfere with his play. A ball so lifted will be replaced after the player has played his stroke.

If a ball in play is accidentally stopped by any outside agency, the ball will be played as it lies, without penalty.

If a ball lodges in anything moving through the green or in a hazard, drop a ball as near as possible to the spot where the object was when the ball lodged in it. On the green, the ball is placed, not dropped. There is no penalty for thus dropping or placing a ball.

However, if a player's ball is stopped or deflected by himself, his partner, or either of their caddies or equipment, the player loses the hole in match play. If a player's ball is stopped or deflected by an opponent, his caddie, or equipment, the opponent's side loses the hole in match play.

If a ball becomes so damaged as to be unfit for play, it may be replaced by another in the spot where the original ball lay. Substitution may be made only on the hole during the playing of which the damage occurred and in the presence of the opponent. Of course, the player may select any ball of his choice to commence play on each hole, and play a different one on each hole if he so elects.

If there is a possibility that a ball is lost or has been driven out of bounds, a provisional ball may be played from the same spot at which the original ball was played (if the original ball was played from the tee, the provisional ball may be played from anywhere within the teeing ground). Through the green or in a hazard the provisional ball is dropped; on the green it is placed. A provisional ball may be played only before a player or his partner goes forward to look for the original ball.

The player may play a provisional ball until he reaches the place where the original ball is likely to be. If the original ball turns out to be actually lost or out of bounds, the player continues to play the provisional ball. If the original ball is found, not out of bounds, the player abandons the provisional ball. If play is continued with the provisional ball, a one-stroke penalty is added.

If a player does not elect to play a provisional ball from the site from which the original ball was stroked, he may drop a ball as close as possible to the spot from which it was originally stroked and add a one-stroke penalty.

(In actual friendly competition, especially on a crowded course, to save time and avoid holding up those playing behind, usually a second ball is dropped at the point where the original ball is presumed to have landed and a one-stroke penalty is added.)

Any movable obstruction may be moved. When a ball is in motion, an obstruction other than an attended flag stick and equipment of the players may not be removed.

When the ball lies on or touches an immovable obstruction or when an immovable obstruction within two club lengths of the ball interferes with a player's stance, stroke, or backward movement of his club for the stroke in the direction he wishes to play, the ball may be lifted without penalty. Through the green or in a hazard the ball will be dropped, or on the putting green placed, within two club lengths of the point outside the obstruction nearest to the point at which the ball originally lay. However, the ball must not come to rest in, on, or touching the obstruction or nearer the hole than it was in its original position.

A ball coming to rest in casual water, ground under repair, or in a hole, cast, or runway made by a burrowing animal, reptile, or bird may be lifted and dropped within a spot as near as possible to the spot where the ball originally lay but not nearer the hole. This applies even in a hazard.

(Casual water is any temporary accumulation of water that is not a hazard of itself or in a water hazard. Snow and ice are considered casual water or loose impediments, at the option of the player.)

A club may not be soled (touch the ground) in a hazard. Penalty: match play, loss of hole; stroke play, two strokes.

In a hazard loose impediments must not be touched, but obstructions may be removed. After a stroke, a player may smooth out irregularities made by footprints or his stroke without penalty, providing nothing is done to improve the lie of the ball or assist the player in his subsequent play of the hole.

A player may have the flag stick attended, removed, or held up to indicate the position of the hole. If the ball comes to rest against the flag stick when it is in the hole, the player may have the flag stick removed, and if the ball falls into the hole, the player is considered to have holed out on this stroke. A player's ball shall not strike the flag stick when it is attended or the flag stick in the hole, unattended, when the ball has been played from the putting green under penalty of loss of hole in match play, two strokes, and the ball to be played as it lies, in stroke play.

CHAPTER TWELVE

Glossary

ADDRESS Position taken by player before making a stroke.

APPROACH A shot played to the green.

AWAY Ball farthest from the hole in play. Player whose ball is away has priority in turn of playing.

BACKSPIN Rotation of ball in flight away from line of flight, imparted by hitting ball on downswing. Backspin causes the ball to stop abruptly or roll only a short distance after landing on the turf.

BIRDIE A hole played in one stroke under par.

BOGEY A hole played in one stroke over par.

BUNKER An area of bare ground that is a hazard, often filled with sand and depressed.

CASUAL WATER Accumulation of water that is not recognized as a hazard.

DIVOT Sod cut with club head during a stroke. All divots should be replaced by the player making them, or by his caddy.

DORMIE In match play, when a player is ahead by as many holes as there are holes remaining to be played, the match is said to be dormie.

DUB An inept golfer. To play a shot badly.

DUFFER An inept golfer.

EAGLE A hole played in two strokes under par. A double eagle (a rare bird indeed) is a hole played in three strokes under par.

FACE Surface of the club head that strikes the ball.

FAIRWAY That portion of ground between tee and green that offers the player a favorable lie for the ball. (In the official rules there is no reference to the fairway or rough. All ground within bounds from tee to green is referred to as "through the green."

FORE A warning cry to a player ahead, or spectator, that a ball is about to be played in his direction or that a ball in flight endangers his safety.

FOURSOME A match in which two players compete against another pair, each side playing one ball. Often confused with a four-ball match, in which each of four players plays a ball.

GIMME Players' slang for a ball so close to the hole that it is conceded by the other side. Not permitted in official medal or stroke play.

GREEN All ground around the cup that has been especially prepared for putting or is designated the putting green.

HALVED When both sides hole out in the same number of strokes, the hole is said to be halved.

HAZARD Any bunker or water or area designated as such between tee and green (except casual water).

HEAD Lower part of the golf club that strikes the ball.

HEEL Point of club at which shaft is fastened to the head.

HOLE Round receptacle on the green into which the ball is played. Also called the cup.

HOLE OUT To put the ball into the cup to complete one unit of play.

HONOR The player or side having priority of play from the tee is said to have the honor.

HOOK A ball that curves to the left of the intended line of flight.

LIE Manner in which a ball in play is resting.

LINKS A term correctly applied only to a seaside course, but generally used in referring to any course.

LOFT Angle at which club face is set from the vertical to raise the ball into the air in flight.

LOOSE IMPEDIMENT Any obstruction not fixed or growing.

MATCH Contest between two or more players or sides.

MATCH PLAY Contest in which winner is determined by number of holes won.

MEDAL PLAY Also called stroke play. Contest in which results are determined by total number of strokes played.

NASSAU A system of scoring widely used for wagering. One point is scored for winning the first nine holes, one point for the second nine, and one point for the eighteen-hole total.

OUT OF BOUNDS Ground on which play is prohibited.

PAR Standard score for a hole.

PENALTY STROKE A stroke added to a score for rule infractions or under certain rules.

PROVISIONAL BALL Ball played after ball previously played has been deemed possibly lost or unplayable.

PULL To hit the ball straight, but to the left of the intended line of flight.

PUSH To hit the ball straight, but to the right of the intended line of flight.

ROUGH Area of long grass, trees, bushes, etc., surrounding fairway from which it is purposely more difficult to make a good shot.

SCLAFF To hit turf behind ball during a stroke.

SHAFT Handle of the club, topped by the grip.

SHANK To hit the ball with socket or neck of club.

SHOT Common synonym for stroke.

SLICE A ball that curves to the right of the intended line of flight.

SOLE Bottom part of club head. Act of placing the club on ground during address.

SQUARE A match that is even is said to be square. Also used with reference to a stance in which both feet are in a line parallel to the line of flight.

STANCE Position of the feet in addressing or stroking the ball.

STROKE Forward movement of the club made with the intention of striking the ball.

STROKE PLAY See Medal Play.

SWING Action of the player in stroking the ball.

TEE Peg, usually wooden, or a mound of sand on which the ball is elevated from the turf for a stroke from the teeing ground.

TEEING GROUND Starting place for the hole to be played. Often referred to simply as the tee.

THREESOME A match in which two players, playing alternate strokes with one ball, oppose a single player, playing one ball. Often confused with a three-ball match, in which three players each play one ball.

TOE Forward part of club head.

TOP To stroke a ball above the center, causing it to hop instead of taking flight in the air.

TWOSOME Often used to designate a single, in which one player competes with another.

WAGGLE Action of flexing the wrists at address, causing the club to move backward and forward preliminary to beginning a stroke.

WHIFF To miss the ball completely on a stroke.

INDEX

Index

Index

Index

BILL MCCORMICK began playing golf many years ago, and not long after, became a sportswriter for the Washington *Post.* In both his game and his writing, he emulated the style of his favorite pros.

He left sportswriting briefly for a public-relations spot in Hollywood, but soon returned to writing for the Scripps-Howard syndicate servicing some seven hundred newspapers, where he also collaborated on an instructional series on sports and aided in the preparation of several golf books by eminent players.

Currently living in France, he has put together in this book the knowledge of golf he has accumulated from great golfers throughout the years.

As Mr. McCormick says, "Had I known when I started everything that is in this book, I probably would have been a great golfer myself. As it is I just dub along as always. But, good or bad, my golf has kept me alive for many years and has been great fun. It always is."